U.S. MARINE CORPS OPERATIONS IN THE DOMINICAN REPUBLIC APRIL - JUNE 1965

by
Major Jack K. Ringler, USMC
and
Henry I. Shaw, Jr.

Occasional Paper

HISTORICAL DIVISION
HEADQUARTERS, U.S. MARINE CORPS
WASHINGTON, D.C. 20380

1970

REPRINTED 1992

This edition published by Books Express Publishing
Copyright © Books Express, 2011
ISBN 978-1-780391-06-9

Books Express publications are available from all good retail
and online booksellers. For publishing proposals and direct
ordering please contact us at: info@books-express.com

Foreword

The history of Marine operations in the Dominican Republic in 1965 is a publication which has had a long but restricted life and it now appears that it would be useful to give it a wider audience interested in an excellent example of the force in readiness concept. The history had its origin in the request of the then-Commandant of the Marine Corps, General Wallace M Greene, Jr., that an account be compiled shortly after the event, when the command diaries of the units involved became available, in the summer of 1965. A classified chronology was prepared using the diaries, message traffic, and other material then available, mostly obtained through the Headquarters Marine Corps Command Center. A narrative was begun once the chronology was completed and several first-hand accounts of the operation had appeared in service publications Particularly useful were the articles "Ubique" by Major General Rathvon McC. Tompkins, the senior Marine officer directly involved, and "Dominican Diary" by Captain James A. Dare, USN, who served as commodore of Amphibious Squadron 10, the Navy organization which transported and landed the 6th Marine Expeditionary Unit, the first American troops ashore The first account appeared in the *Marine Corps Gazette* (September 1965) and the second in the *USNI Proceedings* (December 1965).

The demands of historical reporting and writing about operations in Vietnam caused the incomplete narrative to be set aside until a historian was available to finish it in 1969 It was completed in its present form early in 1970 and distributed as a classified document in February. Years later, the Joint Staff determined that the information contained in the history was no longer classified and copies were placed in the Historical Center Library and made available for inter-library loan. The continuing interest in the operation over the past 27 years prompted a decision to publish the history for wider institutional distribution.

One of the authors, Major Jack K. Ringler, came to the Historical Branch (Historical Division after 1968) following a tour as an infantry officer in Vietnam. He is a graduate of the Naval War College and received a master's degree from George Washington University. He completed this history while serving as the head of the division's reference, archives, and library activities. After his retirement, Major Ringler became a history professor in Nevada. The co-author who began the history and was its overall editor, Mr. Henry I Shaw, Jr., served as a Marine in World War II, obtained a master's degree in history from Columbia University, served again as a Marine in the Korean War, became a Marine Corps civilian historian in 1951, and was chief historian from 1962 to 1990 when he retired

The exacting task of changing the old, much stamped and marked manuscript into the present copy was done by Mrs. Catherine A. Kerns of the Editing and Design Section. In pursuit of accuracy and objectivity, the History and Museums Division welcomes comments on this publication from interested individuals and activities.

E H SIMMONS
Brigadier General
U S. Marine Corps (Retired)
Director of Marine Corps History and Museums

Table of Contents

Table of Contents (Continued)

<u>Maps</u>

U.S. MARINE CORPS OPERATIONS
IN THE DOMINICAN REPUBLIC
APRIL-JUNE 1965

Section 1
Background[1]

The island of Hispaniola, home of two small countries with bloody histories, Haiti and the Dominican Republic (DomRep), occupies a strategic location in the Caribbean Situated close to major shipping lanes to the United States, Europe, and Latin America, Hispaniola lies between Communist-dominated Cuba and Puerto Rico. Within a 1,000-mile radius of Santo Domingo, the capital city of DomRep, are such potential enemy target areas as southern Florida as far north as Cape Kennedy, the Panama Canal, and the oil fields and refineries of Venezuela, Colombia, and the Netherlands West Indies. (See Map 1). Historically, this region has been one of vital interest to the United States--and one in which it has acted unilaterally, at times, to protect that interest.

Since the advent of the Inter-American system, the United States has tried consistently to act in concert with its American neighbors. In pursuit of this goal, it was instrumental in forming, in 1948, the Organization of American States (OAS), a regional agency in terms of the United Nations (UN) Charter, which would deal with such matters relating to the "maintenance of international peace and security as are appropriate for regional action "[2] Meeting at Bogota, Colombia, from 30 March-2 May 1948, the 21 signatory nations of the OAS declared that "an act of aggression against one American State is an act of aggression against all the other American States "[3] They also declared that: "No State or group of States has the right to intervene, directly or indirectly, for any reason whatever, in the internal affairs of any other State" and that: "The territory of a State is inviolable, it may not be the object, even temporarily, of military occupation or of any other measures of force taken by another State, directly or indirectly, on any grounds whatever."[4] Both of these latter statements stemmed in part from a memory of United States' action in the Caribbean in the first three decades of this century, when ships' detachments and Marine expeditionary forces landed repeatedly to protect American lives and property in times of revolution and civil strife. In the 1960s, the heritage left from this era of the "Colossus of the North" and its Marines still had the power to evoke images of intervention--unjustified intervention in the eyes of many Latin Americans.

Against this background, there was ample opportunity for misunderstanding and vehement criticism should the United States feel called upon to use its military forces in any American state without the sanction of the OAS.

A new element entered the picture when Fidel Castro seized control of Cuba in 1959, using a popular revolutionary movement as a means to establish the only Communist-controlled government in the Western Hemisphere. This created a situation of grave peril to the rest of the Americas, whose nations had formally recognized as early as 1948 the interventionist tendency of international Communism and declared it to be "incompatible with the concept of American freedom "[5] Repeatedly over the intervening years, the threat of Communism was the subject of Inter-American debate, criticism, and resolutions of steadfast opposition. When Castro began to give active support to left-wing and Communist elements in other American nations, and to train natives of these countries in guerrilla tactics, subversive activities, and the political techniques that had won him control in Cuba, the situation rapidly deteriorated. At Punta del Este, Uruguay, in January 1962, the OAS excluded the government of Cuba from any participation in the Inter-American system. The foreign ministers of the participating states further recognized that Cuba was accepting "military assistance from extra-continental Communist powers, including even the threat of military intervention in America on the part of the Soviet Union."[6]

The presence of Soviet missiles in Cuba, capable of attacking the U.S., was a danger that none of the American States could ignore. After the U.S. Congress resolved, on 3 October 1962, that the country was determined to "prevent by whatever means may be necessary, including the use of arms, the Marxist-Leninist regime in Cuba from extending, by force or the threat of force, its aggressive or subversive activities to any part of this hemisphere,"[7] the Council of the OAS voted on 24 October "to authorize all collective and individual measures, including the use of force, to halt the flow of aggressive military material to Cuba from the Soviet bloc."[8]

The confrontation between the United States, with OAS backing, and the Soviet Union saw a task force standing by at sea ready to land Marines in assault on Cuban soil and a much larger back-up military concentration in the States ready to move to the attack once the word was given. The U.S.S.R. decision to remove its missiles from Cuba was greeted with a vast sigh of relief from a world on the verge of a global conflict. The lasting effect of that trip to the brink of what could have been nuclear war was a firm United States resolve that there should be no opportunity for another Communist government to come to power in the Americas

The repressive and irresponsible nature of several of the governments of Central and South America gave Communist agents and sympathizers fertile ground for propaganda and subversive action With a history of revolutions, coup d'etats, successive dictatorships, and grinding poverty for the majority of their peoples, these countries had had little opportunity to develop strong representative democratic institutions. Changes of government, when they occurred, did so with often startling rapidity and an accompanying indiscriminate bloodbath that was no respecter of innocent bystanders, native or foreign. In these situations, the ready presence of a hemispheric peacekeeping police force, sanctioned by the OAS, might have helped restore civic order and prevent the senseless destruction of lives and property. But the OAS controlled no such force, nor did it have a military staff to advise it on its use.[9]

Despite the strong language of inter-American agreements against intervention in the internal affairs of any state, if the lives of American citizens were threatened by a sudden flare-up of civil strife in another American nation--and the local organs of public safety were ineffective--the need to act immediately might well outweigh the desire for OAS deliberation and approval of rescue action. Such a situation arose in April 1965, when a revolt in DomRep, centered in Santo Domingo, appeared to present a grave threat to the safety of thousands of foreign nationals in the strife-torn city. Acting on the best intelligence of the situation available to him, President Johnson authorized the landing of U.S. Marines to evacuate their fellow countrymen

Section 2
The DomRep Situation[10]

Hispaniola, discovered by Columbus in 1492, was the site of the first permanent European settlement in the Americas. Spain, and then France, controlled the island in the 17th and 18th centuries. In 1804, the Haitians evicted the French from the western part of the island, and the Dominicans followed suit five years later, wresting control of their country from the French in the name of Spain. In 1821, the Dominicans proclaimed their independence, only to fall victim to a Haitian invasion and occupation which lasted until 1844. Independent again, the Dominicans invited Spain to annex the infant and struggling republic in 1861, but the Spanish withdrew in 1865 when the United States, free from the strains of its Civil War, could turn its attention again to the enforcement of the Monroe Doctrine. (See Map 2)

There was a succession of weak and corrupt governments in DomRep in the years that followed, repeatedly overthrown by revolts, whose promoters and adherents did little to strengthen the nation's economy or the public's well being. The financial situation became so bad, corruption so prevalent, and the debt load so crushing that the United States took control of DomRep customs in 1905, and did not relinquish the hold until 1941. The U.S. imposed an economic council on the republic in 1915, as a result of continual disorder and chaotic mismanagement, and in 1916 instituted a military government backed by a U.S. Marine expeditionary force. When this force withdrew after the election of a constitutional government in 1924, it left behind a well-trained native police force. One of its officers, Rafael Leonidas Trujillo Molinas, an ambitious, ruthless, and talented opportunist, managed to have himself elected President in 1930

During the next 30 years, the Trujillo family and their favored sycophants, particularly the officer corps of the armed forces, systematically ravaged DomRep for their personal gain. While the dictator achieved some measure of economic and administrative stability during his rule, he did so at the expense of the basic human rights of his people. DomRep was a police state, a place of fear and death for any who opposed "The Benefactor of the Republic."

Trujillo was assassinated on 30 May 1961. Only two of the band of 20 conspirators survived the relentless hunt instituted by his son, Air Force General Rafael Trujillo Martinez. Investigators from the OAS said that the widespread repressions were worse than those under his father's rule. The Trujillo hold on the country was crumbling, however, and opposition groups showed themselves boldly for the first time in years. In November, Trujillo's son headed for Europe, his foreign bank accounts filled with his country's treasure When two Trujillo uncles attempted a coup to oust the provisional government, U S warships and transports loaded with Marines appeared offshore and U S. planes flew over the capital city in a show of force. President John F. Kennedy, with the tacit consent of most American governments and the open approval of most Dominicans, interposed U.S. military strength to prevent a reimposition of the old regime. The Trujillos took the pointed hint and fled the country.

.A seven-member interim council, which took office on 1 January 1962, pledged DomRep to active participation in the Alliance for Progress. In effect, a caretaker government was established until elections could be held. During the interval, the council survived one coup attempt by a military-conservative coalition. In December 1962, Juan Bosch of the Dominican Revolutionary Party (PRD) won an election against his nearest rival, Viriato A. Fiallo of the National Civil Union (UCN). Bosch, an exile most of his adult life, and an ardent nationalist with liberal leanings, took office in February in an aura of OAS blessing and firm United States support. He lasted as President about seven months, before he was overthrown by a military coup, sparked by Brigadier General Elias Wessin y Wessin and supported by the conservative elements of Dominican society. These people were disturbed by Bosch's failure to supress communists and fellow travelers, his land and property reform programs, and his drive to cut the strength of the armed forces and reduce the widespread corruption and graft among senior officers.

Reacting to Bosch's overthrow, the U.S. withheld recognition of the civilian junta that took his place until December 1963, when promises of free elections in 1965 were gained. Suspending the 1963 Constitution, which had established the first republican government in DomRep since the rise of Trujillo, the junta ruled by balancing various factions and parties against each other. Promised elections were continually postponed by Donald J. Reid Cabral, the man who became the dominant figure in the ruling group. But Reid's control was far from the dictatorship of Trujillo's day.

The Dominican people, having had a taste of political and personal freedom under Bosch, continually showed themselves to be restive and unhappy about the situation. Plot and counterplot were the order of the day, and a U.S. Army intelligence study examining the period concluded: "It is extremely doubtful that the Dominican Republic, still in a state of political immaturity, will achieve any semblance of political stability in the foreseeable future "[11]

Virtually all DomRep political parties, except the conservative UCN (National Civil Union), were opposed to the Reid government Most active was a coalition of communist and communist-front organizations, the APCJ, MPD, and PSPD,[12] which although outlawed in February 1962 had maintained its strength underground; many of its Castro-trained leaders had returned from exile during Bosch's time in office. Bosch's own PRD, which polled two-thirds of the vote in the 1963 elections, had a strong following in Santo Domingo amongst the lower classes and a growing body of adherents in the armed forces.

Not only did the liberal PRD want Reid overthrown, but so did a number of influential conservatives among the senior officers, the urban upper classes, and the hierarchy of the Catholic Church, all of whom were disturbed at moves that would further disrupt their traditional position of power. American intelligence sources began reporting, early in 1965, the possibility of at least two separate groups attempting a coup against the Reid junta. Fresh rumors of a revolt cropped up continually, but all proved groundless. Thus vague word that another coup was in the making did little to disrupt the plans of the staff of the American Embassy, Santo Domingo, when the weekend of 24-25 April 1965 rolled around

Ambassador William Tapley Bennett, Jr., left for Georgia to visit his mother on the 23d; his ultimate destination was Washington to brief State Department officers on the DomRep situation. Eleven of the 13 officers of the U.S. Military Assistance Advisory Group (MAAG) were in Panama at a regional MAAG conference, and the U S. Naval Attache was off shooting in the country with Brigadier General Antonio Imbert Barreras, one of the surviving Trujillo assassins and a powerful political figure with a reputation as an opportunist. Operations at the Embassy were left in charge of the Deputy Chief of Mission, William Brewer Connett, Jr., a veteran Foreign Service officer.[13]

About noon on Saturday, 24 April, a small group of officers and enlisted men, acting in the name of Juan Bosch, arrested the Army Chief of Staff at his headquarters outside Santo Domingo Reporting the fledgling revolt immediately over a local radio station, the rebels spread the word that Reid was overthrown and people crowded into the streets of Ciudad Nueva, the oldest and poorest section of the capital, shouting: "Bosch! Bosch!" Soon, the main government radio station, Radio Santo Domingo, was denying the report, but PRD supporters seized control of the transmitter and broadcast for two hours that Reid Cabral had fallen, before police broke into their barricaded studio and arrested them.

By now the fat was in the fire. Although Reid Cabral still held nominal power, the streets of Santo Domingo, especially the crowded, lower class sections, were jammed with celebrating PRD supporters and their allies [14] The police, who in general supported the government, were able to drive most of the crowds from the streets by late afternoon and impose a curfew. Reid went on radio and television from the National Palace to broadcast an appeal for calm, to announce that most of the military were with him, and to issue the rebels an ultimatum to lay down their arms by 0500, 25 April, or be annihilated.

The junta leader soon found he was virtually powerless. Aside from the police, he could count on only about 500 troops in Santo Domingo to support him. In contrast, approximately 1,200 soldiers, mainly from Colonel Hernando Ramirez' 16th of August Camp just outside the city, were actively supporting the rebellion An appeal by Reid to General Wessin Y Wessin for support was rejected by the military leader. The general, who commanded the Armed Forces Training Center (AFTC) at San Isidro airbase about eight miles east of Santo Domingo, controlled a mixed force of infantry, armor, and artillery numbering about 1,750 men, which was the best-equipped and -maintained unit of the armed forces.[15]

Although numerous soldiers, some airmen, and almost the whole of the naval frogmen supported the rebels in Ciudad Nueva, the bulk of the armed forces, approximately 18,300 officers and men, were not involved in the initial hours of the revolt in Santo Domingo. Outside the city, where the bulk of the Army's three brigades were stationed and functioning in part as rural police, there was little evidence of an uprising. Although PRD members did approach local garrison commanders to find out their reaction to the conflicting news from Radio Santo Domingo, the almost universal reaction of the military was to wait and see what General Wessin would do. On the 24th he stood pat, no one attacked San Isidro and there is little evidence that troops from San Isidro moved against the rebels in the city.

When it became clear that he could not obtain the support of the armed forces, Reid Cabral and his fellow junta member Ramon Caceres, resigned and were allowed to go into hiding [16] As soon as the word spread by radio and word of mouth, there was frenzied rejoicing in the streets of the capital. As the afternoon wore on armed mobs surged throughout the downtown streets, but as yet there was little bloodshed.

The middle and upper classes, as well as the conservative military leaders at San Isidro, were disturbed at the bizarre sights that filled their television screens. As the rebels took over the government radio and TV facilities, "a constant stream of shouting, weeping, laughing men, women, and children" began appearing on camera, many of them armed and partially in uniform. It was the start of a two-day marathon of such appearances.[17]

The question now beginning to emerge in the minds of the people was what person or persons in the Dominican Republic would assume the reins of government now that the Reid regime had been overthrown . The Boschists demanded the reactivation of the 1963 Constitution and the appointment of PRD leader Rafael Molina Urena as the Provisional President until Juan Bosch could return and assume the Presidency. This was violently opposed by the majority of the military under General Wessin Y Wessin. The military, who had been instrumental in the overthrow of Bosch originally, wanted to establish a military junta. The situation remained pretty much at an impasse until the Air Force Chief, General Juan de los Santos Cespedes, threw his support to the Wessin forces. An ultimatum was given to the Bosch forces to abandon their plans or suffer the consequences This was refused and during the afternoon of 25 April Dominican Air Force planes located at San Isidro took to the air. Four F-51s (single-engine fighters) launched strafing and bombing attacks against the National Palace. Simultaneously Commodore Rivera Caminero, Chief of the Dominican Navy, joined with the Wessin forces and fired several shells into the city from ships offshore.

The air attack on the National Palace changed the tone of the rebel supporters. Trained agitators, believed to have been members of the 14th of June Movement and the PSPD party, incited the people to violence. Earlier that day rebel officers from the 27th of February Camp, located four and a half miles west of the city, broke into the camp's arsenal and loaded several trucks with pistols, rifles, machine guns, and grenades. These arms were then taken into the city where they were distributed to the civilian population. Reinforced with weapons, the civilian population turned into armed mobs and began sacking stores and homes of Trujilloists and triumvirate (junta) supporters. The headquarters of anti-Communist and anti-Bosch parties were set on fire. By nightfall numerous bodies, mostly national police, were lying in the streets and several of the embassies had been hit by small arms fire.

By Monday morning, 27 April, it appeared that Wessin's forces were beginning to take control of the situation. Tanks were moving across the Ozama River, via the Duarte Bridge, which separated San Isidro from Santo Domingo.

This was to be the advance thrust of a coordinated air and naval attack on the central portion of the city held by the rebels.

At this point it appeared the rebels' enthusiasm was beginning to deteriorate as evidenced by the tone of the rebel radio station. Several reasons may have accounted for this feeling: the failure of the revolt to spread throughout the nation; the incessant tension of the past three days, increased by air attacks; and the apparent discouragement among the more responsible rebels at the signs that Communist elements were assuming control of the revolt.

At approximately 1600 on 27 April, rebel President Molina and 20 of his top military and political advisors went to the U S. Embassy, located in the center of the city, to enlist the aid of Ambassador Bennett in ending the conflict. The rebels at this time were ready to agree to a cease-fire, but quickly changed their minds, becoming embittered at what they considered to be Bennett's patronizing and insulting remarks about their irresponsibility for starting the revolt. The Ambassador's words served to strengthen the resolve of the rebels to rally their troops and continue the fight

An uneasy calm settled in Santo Domingo during the early morning hours of the 28th, broken by occasional small arms fire This lull in the fighting may have been due to the conviction of many of the rebel leaders that their cause was lost. Almost all of the responsible leaders belonging to the Bosch PRD party had given up and gone into hiding. Disorder mounted as extremists and Communists gained control as a result of the political disorder which had created a vacuum of authority Confusion and violence increased as the day wore on, with the national police being the targets of the mobs who came from the worker's district in the "old city."

Armed groups roamed the streets, sniping from roof tops, and taking over such government installations as the police stations and the telephone exchange. In an effort to stabilize the situation, a military junta was installed at the San Isidro airfield. This junta was composed of Army, Air Force, and Navy personnel. Late that afternoon the newly formed junta was also on the verge of collapse with many of the officers in a state of hysteria That afternoon the rebels had managed to contain the Wessin attack west of the Duarte bridge. Lack of adequate communications and the inability to consolidate their forces prevented the junta from mounting any type of coordinated offensive.

With Santo Domingo in a state of anarchy and resistance to the mobs crumbling, Ambassador Bennett requested the landing of the Marines. The landing brought an end to the disorder so that by 4 May the Dominican conflict shifted from the military to the political arena. The previous night, ex-President Bosch, from San Juan, renounced his presidential rights in favor of another leader who could become the constitutional president. The next day the rebel coalition announced the formation of a government with Colonel Francisco Caamano as the elected President. Remnants of the Congress that had been elected with Bosch in December 1962, and then ousted, had held a rump meeting attended by some 58 members. Colonel Caamano was chosen by an overwhelming majority to serve as the "Constitutional President" of the Dominican Republic until Bosch's term ran out in February 1967.

To counter the rebels and to gain more popular support, the three-man military junta was disbanded on 7 May and in its place a 5-man civilian-military junta called the National Government of Reconstruction was established The junta was headed by Brigadier General Antonio Imbert Barreras. The other junta members were: Colonel Benoit, the Air Force officer who had headed the outgoing junta; Alejandro Zeller Cocco, a civil lawyer, Dr. Carlos Grisolia Poloney, a lawyer, and Julio D. Postigo, a publisher and editor

These two governments continued to function independently until 3 September 1966 when both sides ceased to exist At this time a Provisional Government headed by Hector Garcia Godoy, a neutral businessman and diplomat from Santiago, assumed control of the government.

Section 3
The Ready Amphibious Task Group[18]

Unstable conditions in the Caribbean Sea area threatening the peace and security of the United States created the requirement for a Ready Amphibious Task Group The Group was established by the Commander in Chief, U.S. Atlantic Fleet (CinCLantFlt) and was composed of Navy and Marine units drawn from the Amphibious Force, U.S. Atlantic Fleet (PhibLant) and Fleet Marine Force, Atlantic (FMFLant). Plans called for the Ready Amphibious Group to be deployed on a continuing basis, conducting such military operations as required to support U.S. policy in the Caribbean area.

The Marine Landing Force consisted of: one battalion landing team (BLT), minus one rifle company based at the Naval Base, Guantanamo, Cuba, as the defense augmentation ready force; one medium helicopter squadron (HMM); one VMF (Fighter Squadron) or VMA (Attack Squadron) based either at the Naval Base, Guantanamo or Naval Air Station, Roosevelt Roads, Puerto Rico; and one VMA or VMF squadron based in the Continental United States (CONUS) on a 24-hour alert. Each deployment was of approximately three months duration with every other BLT and HMM deployment to include a Marine Expeditionary Unit (MEU) Headquarters, Provisional Marine Aircraft Group (ProvMag), and a Logistical Support Unit (LSU) When not employed with the Amphibious Ready Group, the MEU Headquarters remained activated in CONUS prepared for air movement to the Caribbean area to implement contingency plans and other military operations as required.[19]

9

Upon activation, the Ready Amphibious Group, with the Landing Force embarked, was placed under operational control of Commander, Caribbean Sea Frontier (TF 84), and tasked with any or all of the following missions: reinforcement of the Naval Base at Guantanamo; show of force; evacuation of noncombatants; amphibious operations in objective areas assigned, blockade; support of air operations; and furthering Marine operations ashore as assigned.

To formulate detailed plans to meet all the potential contingencies was a virtual impossibility because of the diverse nature of threats to U.S. interests, the widespread area of unrest, and the varied types of military operations envisioned. In order to be prepared for any of these eventualities, the Ready Amphibious Group was directed to conduct maximum training consistent with maintaining readiness for any contingency.

The Marine Landing Force (TG 45.9) of the Ready Amphibious Group composing Carib 2-65 was activated by the Commanding General, FMFLant on 1 February 1965. The Commanding General, 2d Marine Division simultaneously authorized activation of the 6th MEU, designating Colonel George W. Daughtry as the Commanding Officer. Colonel Daughtry was further directed to report to Captain James A. Dare, Commander, Amphibious Squadron Ten (ComPhibGruTen), for planning and subsequent deployment. The 6th MEU was composed of: MEU Headquarters; BLT 3/6 (Lieutenant Colonel Poul F. Pederson), with attached units; LSU (Major Peter L. Stoffelen); ProvMag-60 (Lieutenant Colonel James E. Fegley), including HMM-264 (Lieutenant Colonel Frederick M. Kleppsattel, Jr.), and VMF(AW)-451 (Lieutenant Colonel Dellwyn L Davis), and VMFA-323 (Lieutenant Colonel Norman W. Gourley) as the standby squadrons. VMFA-323 relieved VMA-324, located at the Naval Air Station, Roosevelt Roads, as the MEU standby squadron on 14 March and was in turn relieved by VMF(AW)-451 on 28 April.

The naval units of the Ready Group were formed into Amphibious Squadron Ten, consisting of the helicopter carrier USS *Boxer* (LPH-4), high speed transport USS *Ruchamkin* (APD-89), attack cargo ship USS *Rankin* (AKA-103), amphibious transport, dock USS *Raleigh* (LPD-1), landing ship, dock USS *Fort Snellings* (LSD-30), and the landing ship, tank USS *Wood County* (LST-1178).

The first training exercise involving the Ready Group was QUICK KICK VII. This was a joint Army, Navy, Air Force, and Marine Corps operation, conducted on the island of Vieques, Puerto Rico, and designed to test coordination and control procedures. The 4th Marine Expeditionary Brigade (4th MEB), under the command of Brigadier General John A. Bouker, was activated as the Marine force for the exercise. The majority of the units comprising the MEB were provided by Carib 1-65 (BLT 3/8 and HMM-262), which was already deployed in the Caribbean Sea area, and Carib 2-65 (6th MEU). The two attached helicopter squadrons and the fixed wing squadron were tasked together as part of ProvMag-60. Upon assumption of command by General Bouker, the MEU was deactivated with Colonel Daughtry assuming command of a Regimental Landing Team (RLT). Units from 2d Division Headquarters Battalion and the 2d Service Battalion formed the brigade headquarters and logistic support group (LSG) respectively.

Planning for Operation QUICK KICK VII began on 9 February at ComPhibRon Ten Headquarters with General Bouker, Colonel Daughtry, and Captain Dare attending. Planning continued with 3 April when Carib 2-65 and 4th MEB units departed from Morehead City, North Carolina, for Vieques. Headquarters elements, consisting of 4th MEB Headquarters, ProvMag-60, and LSG Headquarters sailed on board the control ship AGC *Taconic*.

The concept of the operation called for the MEB to conduct an amphibious surface-heliborne assault on the island of Vieques and effect a linkup with Army airborne forces after the seizure of the initial objective. Overall control of the operation was to be exercised by CinCLant through the Commander in Chief, U.S. Army, Atlantic (CinCARLant), who would control the ground operations; Commander in Chief, U.S. Air Force, Atlantic (CinCAFLant), who would control air operations; and CinCLantFlt, who would control both air and ground operations within the Amphibious Objective Area (AOA) through ComPhibGru-Ten and Commander Landing Force (CG, 4th MEB) Upon disestablishment of the AOA, all ground and air operations, less helicopter operations, would revert to CinCARLant and CinCAFLant respectively.[20]

Exercise QUICK KICK VII began at 0630 on 9 April with 4th MEB troops--RLT-6 (BLT 3/8 and BLT 3/6), ProvMag-60 (HMM-262, HMM-264, and VMFA-323), LSG--landing over designated beaches and into landing zones, securing all assigned objectives by that afternoon. Concurrently, the 3d Brigade, 82d Airborne Division was air dropped into the Airborne Assault Area (AAA).[21] At 0730 the next day, RLT-6 continued the attack, seizing all objectives by 0810 At this point all forward movement of the assault companies ceased with the exercise becoming a command past exercise. Late that afternoon after effecting a link-up between BLT 3/6 and the airborne brigade, CG, 4th MEB secured Exercise QUICK KICK VII.[22]

During the course of the exercise, many of the control and coordination areas inherent in a joint operation were tested and a few weaknesses became apparent. Those areas tested, as set forth by CinCLant, were.

1. To exercise and test command and control procedures and techniques while training staffs and participating forces.

2. To exercise and test joint air coordination procedures.

3. To exercise selected reporting procedures for joint operations.

4. To exercise intelligence staffs in all phases of intelligence and to test the expeditious delivery of finished photo intelligence to commanders.[23]

Command and control procedures were considered adequate with one exception CinCLant OpO 10-65 provided for the CG, 4th MEB, when directed by CinCLant, to report "to CinCAFLant for air operations except those involving vertical assault aircraft." It was apparent that the Air Force concept of controlling air in the objective area, once CinCAFLant was established ashore, was to absorb ProvMag-60 into its task organization The drafters of Air Force orders failed to recognize and understand the structure, composition, or mission of a Marine ProvMag. The Air Force was directed by CinCLant to correct the situation, but Air Force orders never completely reflected the change.

Joint air coordination procedures during the exercise proved adequate. Problems which occurred were not the result of the procedures; but rather a lack of discipline, of knowledge of control boundaries, and of inadequate briefings of the pilots. During the course of the exercise, Army, Navy, and Air Force aircraft consistently ignored established procedures for entering the AOA airspaces, thereby greatly endangering the air operations of the Amphibious Task Force On several occasions situations arose which could have resulted in tragic accidents Extreme delays were encountered in heliborne ship-to-shore movements due to these unscheduled flights.

Reporting procedure was considered adequate from the standpoint of the 4th MEB It was recommended, however, that a standard format be established, patterned after the Situation Report (SitRep), to ensure receiving the information desired.

Intelligence problems which beset this exercise were found to be the same as those encountered in DomRep several months later Many of the basic requests for information by units at all levels went unanswered. This was particularly true when requesting up-to-date aerial photography during the movement-to-the-objective phase Many requests, if received at all, were not received in time to be of any use. This was due to the many agencies by which the finished photographs had to be processed before they got to the using agency.

Although not designated as one of the test objectives, civil affairs was found to be a weak link in Marine planning. The 4th MEB had only one civil affairs officer assigned to the staff with all other civil affairs units being constructive. The lack of an overall framework in which to develop civil affairs situations greatly hampered the ability to generate staff play which would have been beneficial to the MEB as well as to the Marine civil affairs officer, as later events proved.

QUICK KICK VII served as a dress rehearsal for the DomRep operation and was invaluable to all concerned. "All the various Navy, Army and Marine staffs were on a first name basis and it assisted immeasurably the orderly phase-in of the various staffs and the coordination between them."[24] Many of the MEB staff officers had participated in exercise GRASS ROOTS in September 1964, materially aiding in solving civil affairs (CA) and psychological warfare (Psy War) command problems. A full awareness of the value of problem situations developed in this exercise was not realized or appreciated until very similar situations arose in DomRep. Both the Marines and the Army were in a much better position to take advantage of each other's capabilities in solving CA and Psy War problems which surfaced during the DomRep crisis. This pointedly substantiated the need for exercises of this type in the future.

Re-embarkation of the 4th MEB was completed on 11 April with 4th MEB units and headquarters augmentation personnel sailing for CONUS. The 6th MEU, reconstituted, steamed for Guantanamo, arriving on 12 April. One company, M/3/6, was landed as the defense augmentation ready force and placed under operational control (opcon) of the Commanding Officer, Naval Base Guantanamo. From 13-16 April, liberty was granted to personnel of the 6th MEU During the period planning began for exercise PLACE KICK, to be held in Vieques, and orientation lectures and trips through Guantanamo defenses were conducted for officers and key staff NCOs.

The efficiency of the Ready Force was further increased when Operation PLACE KICK was conducted on the island of Vieques. This operation was designed to land a joint helo/surface assault force in a fictitious country at the request of the legally constituted, pro-western government in order to restore order and protect U.S. nationals and interests.

The operation began at 0800 on 19 April with Company I/3/6 landing by surface craft across the beach, and Company K/3/6 landing simultaneously by helicopter, followed 30 minutes later by Company L also in helicopters. Shortly thereafter contact among the three companies was established and all objectives were secured. Because of the limited time for training prior to re-embarkation on the 24th, Operation PLACE KICK was terminated at noon so that familiarization firing (FAM) of all weapons organic to the MEU could be conducted. Companies when not actually engaged in FAM firing conducted tactical training at squad and platoon levels. In addition, Fire Support Coordination Center/Field Firing Exercises (FSCC/FFEX) were held, thoroughly exercising the FSCC for the first time. Extensive Forward Air Controller (FAC) team training was also held in cooperation with aircraft from VMFA-323 located in Puerto Rico. Though the training was limited to just three days (20-23 April), it did provide the MEU with valuable experience which better prepared it for contingency operations. Re-embarkation began at noon on the 24th and was completed late that afternoon.

Section 4
Evacuation of U.S. Nationals[25]

The Amphibious Ready Group, having completed re-embarkation at Vieques, was prepared for any eventuality. This force, deployed less than one month, was already a smooth-running, well-coordinated team, which had just completed two amphibious training exercises As preparations were being made to put to sea the next morning to conduct another exercise in the Panama Canal area, events were happening elsewhere in the Caribbean which would bring about a change in these preparations.

The CinCLantFlt Watch Officer at the Command Center in Norfolk began receiving reports late on the evening of the 25th from the U.S. Embassy, Santo Domingo, of riots, demonstrations, and an attempted coup by members of the Dominican Army. This did not come as a surprise as rumors of a coup had been circulating for some time. In accordance with standard procedures, these reports were relayed to the Ready Group for information with instructions that no action was required at that time.

Things rapidly got out of hand during the evening of 24-25 April, with rebel bands attacking the National Police and laying siege to Ozama Fortress. The fortress, one of the major armories in DomRep, bordered the Ozama River about one-half mile south of the Duarte Bridge. A detachment of several hundred white-helmeted, riot control policemen loyal to the deposed government, known as the Cascos Blancos, were defending the fortress against the rebels. The next morning found the city of Santo Domingo without any semblance of law and order. As a result of the deteriorating situation, CinCLant was directed by the JCS to position TG 44.9 off the southwest coast of DomRep, out of sight of land, prepared to evacuate U.S. nationals.[26]

While ships of TG 44.9 were proceeding to DomRep, the JCS in anticipation of a possible troop deployment increased the readiness of the 3d Brigade, 82d AbnDiv, airlift required, close air support elements, command and control headquarters, and support elements for deployment to DomRep.[27]

Ships of TG 44.9, with an evacuation capacity of 3,600 persons, arrived on station early in the morning of 26 April. While en route, the Commanding Officer of 6th MEU issued his warning order for evacuation operations and formulated a plan in conjunction with CTG 44.9 for the protection of U.S. citizens and property.

On Monday evening, 26 April, the American Embassy requested the assistance of Fred Lann, the Assistant Information Officer and an amateur radio operator, in contacting the Ready Group steaming toward Santo Domingo. Lann's radio was the only equipment in the area capable of contacting the Ready Group. Radio communications was first established from Lann's home on the 26th, the day before the evacuation and maintained all during the evacuation. During the early days this was the only link between the carrier *Boxer* and the Embassy. All incoming messages were relayed via telephone to the Embassy until Lann and the Embassy were furnished walkie-talkies for communications. Later when machine gun fire was heard only two doors away, all radio equipment was moved to the house of Public Affairs Officer Malcolm McLean, located several blocks from the Embassy. The next day, 28 April, the radio equipment was again transferred, this time to the Embassy grounds where operations were conducted from Lann's car. This continued for the next four days, until 2 May, when reliable radio equipment was brought ashore.

The Marines brought their own radio equipment with them to the Embassy on the 28th, but to the amazement of all concerned, this equipment could barely be received onboard the *Boxer*. This required the continued use of Lann's equipment for another four days. During the early stages of the operation much of the miscellaneous radio traffic was conducted through ham radio operators located in the DomRep, Puerto Rico, and the U.S.

As confusion and lawlessness mounted during the 26th, the Embassy alerted U.S. citizens to prepare for evacuation, designating the Hotel Embajador as the assembly point and the Port of Haina as the departure point[28]. Later that evening, the Embassy requested the assistance of the U.S. Navy to evacuate U.S. citizens to commence at 0600 the next day. During the night of 26-27 April, U.S. consular officials processed all U.S. nationals who wished to leave the country (See Map 3)

Several members of the diplomatic corps in Santo Domingo also asked for assistance during the initial days of the crisis. At a meeting of the corps on the morning of Thursday, 29 April, the Mexican, Peruvian, Guatemalan, and Ecuadoran Ambassadors voiced concern for the security of their Embassies, Ambassador Bennett offered to evacuate their nationals along with the Americans, an offer which was heartily accepted.

At 0430 on 27 April, elements of the 6th MEU, on board ship, were placed on 15-minute alert to prepare to conduct evacuation operations. In anticipation of the forthcoming orders, a Command Group from the MEU conducted a helicopter reconnaissance of the Haina port area during the early morning hours. Instructions were received from CinCLant at 1157 ordering the ships of TG 44.9 to close and begin evacuation operations, designating San Juan, Puerto Rico, as a safe haven[29]

As TG 44.9 moved within five miles of the DomRep coast, word was received of a disturbing nature. The Embassy reported that a heavily-armed band of rebels invaded the hotel at approximately 1000 on 27 April in search of the owner of the anticommunist newspaper *Prensa Libre*, Rafael Bonilla Aybar, who was reported hiding out in the hotel awaiting evacuation While conducting their search, the rebels terrorized the evacuees by firing their weapons over their heads and threatening to execute the men, eventually leaving when Bonilla could not be found.

That same morning the *Boxer* received word, by message, that Ambassador Bennett would arrive at Punta Caucedo International Airport just outside Santo Domingo. Lieutenant Colonel Kleppsattel (CO, HMM-264), along with Colonel Daughtry, made preparations to meet the aircraft and escort the Ambassador on board the *Boxer*. Taking two UH-1Es over to Punta Caucedo, Lieutenant Colonel Kleppsattel made several low passes over the airfield to insure it was safe before landing. Ten minutes after landing both officers observed an Air Force jet orbiting the *Boxer*. It was felt that the Ambassador was aboard the jet but the pilot was hesitant to land without knowing the airfield was secure Since the operations tower was vacant, Lieutenant Colonel Kleppsattel entered the tower and activated the transmitter, and informed the pilot it was safe to land. After landing, Ambassador Bennett was immediately flown out to the *Boxer* where he conferred with Captain Dare concerning the situation ashore. As the Ambassador was being briefed preparations were made to escort him ashore.[30]

Once the order was given to commence evacuation operations, a beach control unit from the LSU, a pathfinder element from HMM-264, an air control element from ProvMag-60, and two unarmed squads from K/3/6 were launched by helicopter to the Port of Haina. The beach control unit, assisted by one squad from K/3/6, was to coordinate evacuee loading on board the LST *Wood County* and APD *Ruchamkin*, tied alongside the Haina pier. The pathfinder element and the air control element, assisted by the other squad from K/3/6, were to establish a landing zone for helicopter evacuation to the LPH *Boxer* and LPD *Raleigh*.[31]

The first convoy consisting of trucks, buses, and embassy vehicles began leaving the hotel around 1300. The *Ruchamkin* and *Wood County* completed the loading of 620 passengers by 1630, and sailed immediately for San Juan. While the *Ruchamkin* and *Wood County* were moving to the Haina pier, the pathfinders had marked out the helicopter landing zone (LZ-6) near the port.[32] A total of 16 UH-34s were used in the lift and by 1820 a total of 264 evacuees had been lifted on board the *Raleigh* and 294 on board the *Boxer*[33]

A final reconnaissance of the Haina port area was conducted by the 6th MEU Command Group shortly after the last helicopter cleared the area to ensure

16

that no stragglers were left behind. During the day's operations, HMM-264 logged 59 hours in 102 sorties and evacuated 558 civilians. This was only a prelude of what the pilots would experience during the next few weeks.[34]

That evening, while the flagship was preparing to get underway for San Juan, orders were received to retain the *Boxer* in the area: With the change of orders, plans had to be made to transfer the 294 passengers from the *Boxer* to the *Raleigh*. The move was postponed until the next morning since the physical condition of the women and children was bordering on exhaustion. At 0900 on 28 April, the transfer began by helicopter and was completed shortly before noon. With the transfer completed, the *Raleigh* got underway for San Juan.

Back in Santo Domingo on the morning of the 28th the streets were again filled with rebels, to the complete surprise of everyone because of their apparent collapse the night before. They turned the downtown business district of Santo Domingo and the maze of narrow streets in the old part of the capital into their main stronghold. Earlier that morning, the forces under Wessin announced the formation of a military junta in the absence of any legitimate government in Santo Domingo. This was done in response to urging by the U.S. Embassy. The junta consisted of three members, one from each of the Dominican Armed Forces, with Colonel Benoit as President

At 1400, the U.S. Embassy received a call from Junta President Benoit requesting the Embassy to land 1,200 Marines to "help restore peace in this country." At this time Ambassador Bennett was of the opinion that the situation did not warrant such action. It was not until increased sniper fire was reported around the Embassy and Embajador Hotel, later that afternoon, that Ambassador Bennett asked Washington to land the Marines to insure the safety of the evacuees and to reinforce the Marine guard at the Embassy.[35]

All through that day a steady stream of U.S. and foreign nationals had been converging at the Embajador Hotel to await evacuation. Late that afternoon the Embassy was informed by the national police that they could no longer provide protection along the evacuation route to Haina In view of this alarming news the Ambassador, at 1730, requested evacuation operations be transferred from Haina to the Embajador Hotel.

Plans changing the evacuation point were put into effect immediately. The speed by which this was accomplished was due primarily to the close liaison maintained between the Embassy and the 6th MEU. Those reports received by the Embassy earlier that day had been passed to Colonel Daughtry. In anticipation of any eventuality, the battalion had been placed on alert at 1615 and positioned at the hanger deck Upon receipt of the Ambassador's request a pathfinder element and an unarmed platoon from Company K were in the air in a matter of minutes. These units were to establish a landing zone (LZ-4) in the polo field located next to the Embajador Hotel and to assist in evacuation operations.[36] The pathfinder element landed in the first four helicopters, followed by the platoon from Company K. Shortly after the arrival of the first helicopters, civilian evacuees began arriving by automobiles in the landing zone where they were flown out to the awaiting ships.

After debarking the first evacuees, the helicopters loaded and transferred the 2d Platoon, Company L, reinforced with two squads, ashore to augment the Marine guard at the Embassy. Upon arrival the platoon boarded waiting civilian vehicles for transfer to the Embassy where they were deployed around the main Embassy building.

While these units were en route to the landing zone, the JCS directed CinCLant to take the necessary action to land the battalion landing team from the *Boxer* and to place two Army Airborne Battalion Combat Teams (BCTs) in a DefCon-2 status.[37] In response to this directive, CinCLant ordered Captain Dare to land the Marines if requested by the Ambassador. After a brief consultation between Ambassador Bennett and Colonel Daughtry, it was decided to land the Marines in order to protect U.S. lives and property.[38]

Further preparations were made as ComCaribSeaFront ordered VMFA-323, located at Roosevelt Roads to prepare four aircraft with air-to-air and air-to-ground ordnance for possible missions over DomRep. The alert status was later changed to unarmed strip alert on the night of 28-29 April and armed strip alert for eight aircraft by 0345 on the 29th.[39]

Having been previously alerted, the remainder of Company L, less the ship's platoon, was lifted into LZ-4 at dusk. By the time the helicopters reached the LZ it was completely dark and beginning to rain. Immediately upon landing the company spread out, establishing a defensive perimeter in preparation for the landing of the rest of the BLT located on board the *Boxer*.

That night BLT 3/6 conducted a vertical assault under combat conditions during the hours of darkness. As the weather became progressively worse, HMM-264 shifted into a tight diamond formation during the approach instead of the unwieldy tactical formation. This weather required the pilots to fly by instruments between the LZ and the *Boxer* located 15 miles offshore.

The last flight of helicopters returned to the *Boxer* shortly before midnight. The aircraft of HMM-264 performed double duty that night, transporting 536 Marines and 18 tons of equipment ashore, returning with 684 civilians. Those forces transported ashore included the Alpha Command Group (Lieutenant Colonel Pederson) and BLT 3/6 consisting of: Company L (-); Company K (-); and H&S Company (-). This amounted to a total strength of 30 USMC officers, 478 USMC enlisted, 2 USN officers, and 22 USN enlisted. The pilots of

HMM-264 had logged closed to eight hours of almost continuous flying time of which five and a half hours was during darkness under very hazardous conditions.

That morning the perimeter had only included the landing zone. With the large number of evacuees at the Embajador Hotel it was decided that evening to extend the perimeter and accordingly orders were issued extending it to include the hotel. A roadblock was established at the road leading into the hotel from the north to prevent the entry of any armed rebels that might be in the area

Shortly after midnight Embassy officials urgently requested medical supplies and additional Marines to protect the Embassy. Lieutenant Colonel Pederson dispatched a 27-man "clutch" platoon composed of personnel from H&S company under the command of Master Sergeant Harold E. Lanter The platoon departed for the Embassy in civilian vehicles escorted by Commander Richard Holmes of the MAAG The medical supplies arrived early the next morning and were issued to Red Cross and civilian medical agencies in coordination with Embassy officials.

At the first light on the 29th, helicopter operations began with two UH-1Es of HMM-264 lifting members of the 6th MEU Command Group into the Embassy compound for a conference with Embassy officials. At the direction of the Embassy, 4,000 MCI rations were ordered delivered to the Dominican Air Force at San Isidro as supplies to the airfield had been cut off by the rebels. Eight UH-34s were launched to conduct the supply missions between the *Raleigh/Boxer* and Red Beach/LZ-4/San Isidro airfield, and to continue evacuation operations. All helo operations stopped at 1915 after a total of 516 evacuees had been lifted during the day.

When it had become apparent that a landing was going to take place, the *Raleigh* was recalled from San Juan where it had been disembarking evacuees. Arriving in the area on the 29th, the *Raleigh* now took on added importance since it was carrying the remaining company (Company I) together with the heavy equipment of the BLT. This gave the landing force commander flexibility in determining by what method Company I would be landed: LVT or helicopter. The problem that emerged was what method would be the best. If the units ashore became engaged, Company I could be heli-lifted into any portion of the perimeter to reinforce the BLT. This might require, however, the use of naval gunfire and tactical air support, a type of escalation not desired. Additionally, if the BLT was ordered to expand the present perimeter using helicopters, the forces ashore would be at a disadvantage if serious opposition should develop as both methods would leave the BLT without its heavy equipment. This would require the landing of such equipment at Haina and an overland movement north to join the rest of the battalion, a hazardous journey since it would allow the rebels the opportunity to choose the time and place for an attack

This problem was solved with the formulation of Operation BARREL BOTTOM. When Company I was ordered ashore, the company together with the heavy equipment of the battalion would move by landing craft across Red Beach.[40] Upon completion of the landing, all units were to form up into an armored column and move up the highway to make a juncture with the rest of the BLT at the Embajador Hotel. The supporting elements of the Navy remaining at Haina would constitute the logistical tail for the BLT.

That afternoon, Captain Dare and Colonel Daughtry decided to go ashore and obtain first-hand information because of conflicting reports received from units ashore. A meeting was arranged for that afternoon between the Ambassador and the two military commanders to discuss and evaluate the situation. Reports previously received indicated the situation was somewhat stabilized. These reports proved in error when further discussions with Embassy staff members and military attaches revealed that the rebels were expanding their operations while loyalist forces were stalled. As a result, Ambassador Bennett was prompted to request the two alerted Abn BCTs be moved to DomRep and the remainder of the 6th MEU be landed from the *Boxer*.

That afternoon, Captain Dare was given the order to land the remainder of the 6th MEU. The two Abn BCTs, located at Fort Bragg, North Carolina, were to be flown to Ramey AFB, Puerto Rico, prepared for an air-assault drop near the San Isidro airfield early on 30 April.

While returning to the Boxer, the two commanders gave the order to begin Operation BARREL BOTTOM. Late that afternoon, Company I with two sections of 106mm recoilless rifles, together with tanks, Ontos, and LVTs located aboard the *Raleigh*, *Wood Count* and *Fort Snelling*, began landing across Red Beach. Immediately after landing, the units formed into an armored column and moved north to join the rest of the BLT at the Embajador Hotel, arriving at 1830 EST.[41] With the arrival of the units from Haina, the perimeter around the Embajador Hotel was strengthened and by nightfall the BLT occupied a 360-degree defense perimeter with a strong reserve.

Section 5
POWER PACK Build-up[42]

During the Dominican Crisis the decision-making process was physically concentrated in the White House and the State Department. The participants included the President, the Secretary of Defense, the Secretary of State, the Under Secretary of State for Economic Affairs, the Director, CIA, the Chairman of the Joint Chiefs of Staff, and special assistants from the White House and

State Department. The Chairman of the Joint Chiefs was the only military representative of the decision-making group and, as such, spoke for the Joint Chiefs of Staff.

This group was compelled in the initial period to make decisions on the basis of very inadequate and often contradictory intelligence on the issues at stake in the revolt. The primary source of information was the Ambassador in Santo Domingo and decisions depended upon the Ambassador's judgment and his estimate of the situation. There existed continuous demands from the decision-makers for detailed information of all aspects of the operations because of the tight military control over deployments

The establishment of a joint task force within the Atlantic Command, known as Joint Task Force 122, had been planned to meet such contingencies in the Caribbean Sea area. This force was to be commanded by Commander Second Fleet in addition to his other duties Commander Joint Task Force 122 (CJTF-122) had the responsibility for the preparation of operation plans in support of the overall CinCLant plans The forces making up JTF-122 were to be made available by CinCLant. Once ordered activated, augmentation personnel for the staff were to be provided by CinCLant on an additional duty basis for planning and on a temporary basis for operations. When augmentation requirements exceeded CinCLant's capabilities, additional personnel were to be requested from the appropriate service or agency [43]

The military planning for contingencies in DomRep was contained in CinCLant OPlan 310/2 This plan was approved by the JCS on 19 January 1962 and provided for the introduction of U.S. forces into DomRep in the event that the government in office became hostile to the aims and objectives of the US/OAS, or upon the outbreak of severe internal disorders, or upon the request of the government or a group claiming to exercise authority in DomRep. Although the JCS did not order execution of OPlan 310/2, it was used by subordinate commands as basic guidance during the DomRep crisis.

Once the situation in DomRep began to deteriorate, action was initiated by CinCLant on 26 April to form Joint Task Force 122. JTF-122 was given the mission to protect American lives and effect evacuation of U.S. and foreign nationals if requested by the U.S. Ambassador in DomRep. Two days later, JTF-122 was formally activated under the command of Vice Admiral Kleber S. Masterson. Admiral Masterson with his Deputy, Major General Rathvon M. Tompkins, and a small staff of nine officers departed Norfolk, Virginia, by air for Ramey AFB, Puerto Rico, during the early hours of the 29th. After a short briefing at Ramey by Rear Admiral Henry H Caldwell (ComCaribSeaFron), CJTF-122 boarded the DD *Leahy* for further movement to DomRep Arriving off the coast of Santo Domingo that afternoon, CJTF-122 shifted his flag on board the *Boxer* and assumed command.

Admiral Masterson was briefed by Captain Dare and Colonel Daughtry as to the status of forces and situation ashore and the progress of the evacuation effort. At the time TG 44.9 was deactivated and TF-124 was activated in its stead with Captain Dare as the commander until 4 May when Vice Admiral John S. McCain (ComPhibLant) assumed command. JCS assigned the unclassified code name to the operation in DomRep of POWER PACK.

Two airborne BCTs which had been placed in a DefCon 2 status on the 28th departed Pope AFB the next evening and while airborne were diverted from Ramey to San Isidro, where they were ordered to be air-landed instead of air-dropped. Previously it had been uncertain whether the airfield was in the hands of friendly forces. Upon receiving a report that General Wessin Y Wessin, commander of the forces at San Isidro, was in the area near the Embajador Hotel, an officer and a Spanish-speaking sergeant from MEU Headquarters were sent ashore to locate and bring General Wessin onboard the *Boxer* for a conference. It turned out the only general in the area was General Imbert, who came in Wessin's place: After a brief conference, Admiral Masterson was assured by General Imbert that the airfield was under the control of the loyalists and that it would be safe to land aircraft. General Imbert pointed out, however, that the control tower was not in operation during the hours of darkness. This information was passed to the JCS and the decision was then made to divert the two BCTs to San Isidio. Lieutenant Sam H. Hawkins, USN (CJTF's aide), Captain Harrison W. Kimbrell, USMC (General Tompkin's aide), and Captain Taylor, USMC (on staff of Phibron-10) were directed by Admiral Masterson to go ashore and take over control of the tower in order to assist in the landing of aircraft bringing in the airborne troops.

The 3d Brigade (two BCTs) of the 82d Airborne Division, onboard C-130s, began arriving shortly after midnight. Their landing was assisted by Lieutenant Hawkins and Brigadier General Robert L. Delashaw, USAF (CTF-121) who directed the Airborne Direct Air Support Center. All aircraft were landed without a mishap, despite the heavy air traffic in an area unfamiliar to the pilots.

Major General Robert H. York, USA, Commanding General of the 82d AbnDiv, landed with the lead plane. The first order of business was the unloading of the aircraft which had been rigged for an air drop. This was a long and back-breaking job and had to be done by hand because of a lack of materials-handling equipment. General York stayed only long enough to insure the unloading was proceeding as rapidly as possible, whereupon he helicoptered to the *Boxer* for orders. Admiral Masterson designated General York as the commander of all ground forces (CTF-120) in the Santo Domingo area.[44]

Early in the operation it was found necessary by CinCLant to activate ARLant and AFLant in order to assist in the daily coordination of plans, operations, and logistics. CinCAFLant was designated as the air component commander for operations connected with DomRep and to prepare for the control and movement of designated forces to DomRep On 1 May, Major General Marvin L. McNickle, USAF, assumed command of CTF-121 with General Delashaw becoming his deputy.

In response to a JCS directive, Admiral Masterson, on 30 April, prepared his initial concept for operations ashore, informing CinCLant of his plans. This plan called for the 3d Brigade to secure the airfield, screening the east and north from rebel fire. The brigade, minus the screen and security forces, was to move to an assembly point west of the airfield to effect a relief of loyal DomRep forces, secure the Duarte Bridge, and establish a cordon and roadblocks east of the Ozama River.

The 6th MEU was to leave a detachment at LZ-4 to secure the landing zone and move west to establish an International Safety Zone (ISZ) from the sea north along Calle Socorro Sanchez, Calle Navarro, and Avenida Presidente Rios to the juncture at Avenida San Martin. (See Map 2)

U.S. forces were directed to use no weapons larger than small arms, unless authorized by higher headquarters. Loyal DomRep forces were to patrol the area between U.S Army and Marine perimeters.

General Tompkins, together with General York, was dispatched to the U.S. Embassy to obtain the concurrence of Ambassador Bennett for Admiral Masterson's concept. After the conference, Ambassador Bennett requested both generals to meet with members of the junta to secure their acceptance to the plan The meeting was held at junta headquarters at San Isidro After a long discussion, Colonel Benoit, President of the Junta, agreed to the plan.[45]

By midmorning of 30 April, the 3d Brigade (-) began its movement towards the Duarte Bridge, receiving light sniper fire as it approached the east side of the bridge. Flanking elements were immediately deployed to the south, clearing their area of the rebels. Four members of the brigade were wounded during the action. By late afternoon the relief of the junta forces was effected and the brigade assumed responsibility for the bridgehead. Junta forces that were to patrol the area between the Army and Marine perimeters moved back to the safety of the airfield leaving the Army and Marine units isolated from each other.

While the Army units were moving towards the bridge, BLT 3/6 was directed by Colonel Daughtry to move eastward to positions beyond the U.S. Embassy and occupy strongpoints along a phase line (CAIRO). The western portion of Santo Domingo, the area to be known as the International Safety Zone (ISZ) which was to be secured by the Marines, contained many more rebels than did the 3d Brigade's area in the east Expecting heavier resistance Marine units were preceded by tanks, Ontos, and LVTs. Truckloads of Marines moved eastward in a three-pronged advance from the Embajador Hotel staging area to Abraham Lincoln Avenue, the Marine Line of Departure (LOD) for phase line CAIRO. After crossing the LOD, the three companies advanced in a single file, hugging garden walls and moving from tree to tree and from telephone pole to telephone pole. The battalion commander and his S-3 (Major Henry V. Martin) observed the movement from an observation UH-1E helicopter which enabled them to communicate with units on the ground and MEU Headquarters onboard the *Boxer*.

The battalion began its advance shortly before noon. Captain William G. Davis' Company I moved out along the left boundary (north) of the zone of advance (ZOA) to phase line CAIRO and established checkpoints at objectives "C" and "D."[46]

As Company I was approaching objective "C," it began to receive rebel small arms fire from the old Santo Domingo airport, where low-income houses were being built, and from the buildings along Avenida Presidente Rios, between objectives "C" and "D." Captain Davis requested permission at this point to use heavier caliber weapons to dislodge the rebel force This required the request to be forwarded up the chain of command, and it was not until 1530 that authorization was granted and then only for the use of 3.5-inch rocket launchers.

Upon reaching objective "C," Captain Davis established a base of fire with the 2d Platoon (First Lieutenant Kenneth E. Bailey) and maneuvered the 1st Platoon (First Lieutenant Thomas E. Clinton) to the northeast to be in position to attack the housing project in the west. As the 1st Platoon was moving into position it came under heavy rebel fire from the housing project, and from buildings in the vicinity of objective "D" and those bordering the northwest side of Avenida San Martin. With the platoon pinned down by the heavy cross-fire, Lieutenant Clinton ordered a withdrawal by LVTs. During this engagement the 1st Platoon sustained four wounded casualties.

Captain Davis realized the housing project to the northwest had to be cleared in order for objective "C" to be tenable. To accomplish the task, the 2d Platoon advanced by a series of squad and fire team rushes, supported by machine gun fire. This action proved sound as the objective was successfully cleared of all rebel opposition. The rebels were observed withdrawing from the area, carrying their wounded with them. Two dead were found in the area.

With the taking of objective "C," the 3d Platoon (First Lieutenant George E. Kallen) with the support of two LVTs and one tank advanced to the north to

24

seize objective "D." As the platoon advanced, rebel fire was immediately received from buildings in the vicinity of the objective, increasing as the platoon reached the objective. Since authorization had not yet been received for the use of larger caliber weapons, the 3d Platoon was ordered to withdraw. When authorization was received that afternoon to use 3.5-inch rocket launchers, they were immediately placed in position and used with extremely effective results. Approximately 30 rounds were fired, which succeeded in reducing the volume of fire to sporadic sniping. Rebels were observed withdrawing to the north. The 3d Platoon sustained five casualties during the action· one killed and four wounded.

It became apparent to the company commander that the occupation of objective "D" would require many troops to occupy the buildings in and around the area in order to deny their use by the rebels. In view of this, Captain Davis recommended that objective "D" not be occupied at this time. This recommendation was forwarded up the chain of command to Colonel Daughtry who concurred, directing that the company consolidate its position at objective "C." Three roadblocks and one checkpoint were established, with limited combat patrols being sent out periodically to prevent snipers from returning close to the company's positions.

Company K, under the command of Captain Robert C. Cockell, crossed the LOD shortly after Company I, advancing in the center portion of the ZOA to phase line CAIRO, with the mission of establishing a roadblock at objective "B."[47] The advance was conducted without opposition, and it was not until later that evening that sniper fire was received in the company's positions. This rebel fire came from the buildings located to the north in the same area from which Company I had previously received sniper fire. The rest of the 30th proved uneventful and the 3d Platoon was detached and moved to the U.S Embassy to assist in its perimeter defense.

The movement of Company L, under the command of Captain Horace W. Baker, assigned the southern portion of the ZOA, also proved to be without opposition. Arriving at objective "A," the company set up one roadblock and established contact with Company K to the north [48]

Once in position, the company began receiving increasing sniper fire Headquarters personnel from the company, under the command of First Lieutenant Thomas Taylor, were ordered to clear the buildings around the CP, an action which resulted in the killing of one rebel. In order to control the east-west movement along the George Washington Highway and the beach, the company extended its position south along Calle Sanchez to the junction at George Washington Highway

As the companies were moving to the phase line, Major Joseph J. Gambardella, the battalion executive officer, was sent to effect liaison with the National Police and Dominican troops positioned in and around the National Police building. After apprising officials of the battalion's actions, Major Gambardella attempted to obtain their assistance in the control of roadblocks and checkpoints in order to keep the "trigger happy" police from firing into Marine positions. Officials were willing to furnish troops along the phase line, but were afraid that any troops at the roadblocks and checkpoints would only draw rebel fire. They did, however, provide interpreters at these points.

Around noon Lieutenant Colonel Pederson and Major Martin returned from their helicopter reconnaissance of the area and moved by LVT from LZ-4 to the U.S. Embassy. After making an estimate of rebel activity around the Embassy, the battalion commander was prompted to move the battalion CP within the grounds. This gave the commander a more central location in directing the battalion's forces, maintained immediate contact with the Embassy, and provided additional protection to the Embassy by the CP group. Once the battalion CP was established at the Embassy grounds, the Alpha Command Group was moved from objective "A" where it had displaced temporarily earlier that morning. The operations center was established in the command LVT where the processing, consolidating, and issuing of orders to subordinate units was conducted. The LVTs during the day were utilized in a supply role transporting supplies from Haina and LZ-4 to the Embassy.

One section of 106-mm recoilless rifles was attached late that afternoon to Companies K and L, giving all three companies the same antitank capability. With the coming of darkness, the battalion was now prepared for any eventuality. Throughout the night the battalion was to receive harassing fire from snipers, an occurrence which the Marines would experience throughout their stay in DomRep. As the troops became accustomed to this sniping fire there was an improvement in the fire discipline. Initially rebel fire was returned in many instances by Marines without their having a suitable target.

With Marine units now located in the west and Army units in the eastern portion of Santo Domingo, Admiral Masterson became concerned over the absence of physical contact between the two. Junta forces had agreed, on 30 April, to occupy a cordon area between the two. Once the Army moved into the area around Duarte Bridge, however, the junta forces retired to the safety of San Isidio. To correct this situation, it was decided to effect a linkup on 1 May. Company I/3/6 and elements of the 3d Brigade, 82d AbnDiv were given the mission. Liaison was effected quickly and easily, based on the experience gained by the same two units who had operated together a few weeks previously during exercise QUICK KICK VII.

Company I moved east from objective "C," while an armored column of approximately 200 men from the 3d Brigade moved west from the Duarte Bridge. The Marines encountered no resistance during their eastward movement. This was not the case for the Army column led by Lieutenant Colonel George C. Viney, Commanding Officer, 3d Brigade. During the move the brigade sustained four casualties: two killed and two wounded by sniper fire. The linkup of the two columns was effected at 1253 in the field next to an open air theater, located on Avenida San Martin, between Calles Manuel Gomez and Marcos Adon. The combined forces patrolled the immediate area and then, at 1545, they were ordered by General York to return to their original positions.

With the activation of the XVIII Abn Corps on the afternoon of the 30th, General Bruce Palmer and members of his staff departed CONUS that same day. Arriving at San Isidro at 2345 that night General Palmer assumed command of TF-120 and of all ground forces in DomRep. The remaining BCTs and brigade headquarters of the 82d AbnDiv and the 101st AbnDiv were placed on DefCon 3.[49]

Upon his arrival, General Palmer was faced with the problem created by the separation of Marine and Army units. It became increasingly apparent that with the increase of U.S. forces in DomRep a security corridor/line of communications (LOC) would be required in order to capitalize on the use of the port at Haina and the airfield at San Isidro. This division of forces became so intolerable, that on 2 May, the JCS directed the forces ashore to establish such a corridor. Given the code name BLUE CHIP, the operation called for one platoon from I/3/6 to advance east along Calle Juan Bosco to Calle Rosa Duarte. Airborne infantry units were to move west from the Duarte Bridge, along Avenida Garcia. The move was planned as a night operation to avoid the involvement of innocent civilians as well to surprise any rebels in the area. The entire operation was completed in one hour and 11 minutes without incident. Operation BLUE CHIP bisected the city, splitting the rebels in two. The rebel's main stronghold and the capital's business district was, in effect, surrounded by U.S. forces Several days later, on 5 May, the main axis of the corridor was expanded two blocks on each side in order to protect convoys from sniper fire.

In anticipation of a possible buildup, as developed several days later, the CG, 2d MarDiv activated the 4th MEB headquarters on 29 April. FMFLant designated the major forces of the MEB to consist of: 4th MEB Headquarters; 6th Marines; BLT 1/6, BLT 3/6, and BLT 2/2 which was later replaced by BLT 1/2; and ProvMag-60, to include HMM-263, HMM-264, VMFA-323, and VMF(AW)-451. In response to a JCS directive, CinCLant ordered the deployment of the MEB Headquarters and 1/6 by air and 1/2 by surface craft. The 2d Brigade (two BCTs of the 82d AbnDiv) was to deploy from Fort Bragg as soon as possible The three remaining BCTs of the airborne division were placed in an optimum posture for rapid deployment.

With the activation of the 4th MEB, ComPhibLant was directed to sail the LPH *Okinawa* to Onslow Beach, near Camp Lejeune, to embark BLT 1/2 and HMM-263. Simultaneously, PhibRons 8 and 12 sailed for Morehead City/Onslow Beach to embark the seatail of the 4th MEB Headquarters and the combat support units of BLT 1/2 respectively. BLT 1/6's support units accompanied it on board the aircraft. Arriving off Santo Domingo between 4-6 May, BLT 1/2 was assigued opcon to 4th MEB and given missions as MEB reserve and interim relief Ready Force. The battalion remained on board ship during the entire crisis as the requirement for a reserve force ashore never materialized.

The 2d Marine Division, in anticipation of such contingencies as developed in the DomRep, was tasked with maintaining an airlift alert battalion capable of being air transported beyond the continental limits of the United States to conduct military or such other operations as might be required. The outbreak of the DomRep crisis found the 1st Battalion, 6th Marines standing in an alert status, having been designated as the airlift battalion on 23 April. The Alpha increment (Company C) was directed on the evening of 28 April to proceed from Camp Lejeune to Cherry Point and load onboard waiting C-130 aircraft. Later that night orders were received from the division to hold at the air station, and the troops were unloaded and billeted near the airfield. After several changes of orders, the Alpha increment was finally directed to board the aircraft for transfer to the U.S. Naval Base, Guantanamo Bay, Cuba. Upon arrival in Cuba, the company was transferred to the DD *Roan* and DLG *Luce*, and set sail immediately for DomRep. Arriving at the Port of Haina early in the morning of 30 April, the troops disembarked from the ships to waiting trucks for the move to the Embajador Hotel. The Alpha increment was placed under opcon of BLT 3/6 and assigned to defensive positions around the hotel and polo field.

That morning, while Company C was moving into its defensive positions, the remainder of BLT 1/6, under the command of Lieutenant Colonel William F. Doehler, departed Camp Lejeune for Cherry Point. Orders were received at 1115 on 1 May to airlift the Bravo (Battalion Headquarters and Company B) and Delta (Company D) increments immediately, with Charlie (Detachment H&S, Tactical Air Control Party), Echo (Company A), Foxtrot (H&S Company), and Golf (Miscellaneous) increments to follow as soon as aircraft became available. Also embarked on the first outgoing aircraft was General Bouker, Commanding General, 4th MEB and selected members of his staff.

General Bouker, arriving late the afternoon of 1 May, reported to Admiral Masterson onboard the *Newport News* where he was placed in command of all Marine forces in DomReP. Also at this time the MEU was redesignated as RLT-6 and ProvMag-60 was tasked organized under the MEB. The CP for the MEB was established initially onboard the *Boxer*, and was then moved ashore on 2 May to the Hispaniola Hotel, located at the southern end of Calle Juan Thomas Diaz.

Lieutenant Colonel Doehler landed at San Isidro airfield early the evening of 1 May. Utilizing the communications equipment of the 82d Division, arrangements were made with RLT-6 to move the battalion to LZ-4. The remainder of the battalion landed intermittently throughout the night at San Isidro in "bits and pieces." This was the result of ignoring unit integrity in outloading from Cherry Point. By 0602 on 2 May, however, the battalion, less Company C, was reassembled

At 0725 on 2 May, UH-34D helicopters from HMM-264 began arriving from the *Boxer* for the lift of BLT 1/6 from San Isidro to LZ-4. Late that evening, Major Sam G. Olmstead, S-3 of RLT-6, arrived at the polo field by helicopter to deliver the operation order for the next day Lieutenant Colonel Doehler's battalion was given responsibility for the center portion of the ISZ bounded by Avenida Abraham Lincoln, Pedro Henriquez Urena, Maximo Gomez, and the sea to the south, with added instructions to pay close attention to the northern portion of the boundary. The battalion had the additional assignment of providing security for the MSR from the Beach Support Area at Haina to the western boundary of 3/6's positions, and of providing one company for the regimental reserve In anticipation of the move, a helicopter reconnaissance was conducted during the evening and morning of 2-3 May by Major Karl E. Moore (Battalion S-3 of 1/6) to select a centrally located CP. The site chosen was at the intersection of Avenida Paulo III and Calle Nunez de Cacres in that part of Santo Domingo known as University City.

With the departure of BLT 1/6 for DomRep, the 1st Battalion, 8th Marines was designated as the airlift alert battalion Under the command of Lieutenant Colonel Edward F Danowitz, the battalion began immediate preparations for a possible move to the south. As the situation continued to deteriorate, the various increments of the battalion were advanced in conditions of readiness. The battalion was directed by the CG, 2d MarDiv on 2 May, to move to Cherry Point, with the first increment departing shortly after midnight onboard C-130s for San Isidro The leading elements of the battalion consisting of Lieutenant Colonel Danowitz and Company D touched down at the airfield at 0520 on 3 May. By 2100 that evening the entire battalion was in Santo Domingo, billeted just outside the main gate of the San Isidro airbase.

Space became a premium at the polo field during the morning of 3 May as leading elements of 1/8 began arriving in the area to replace 1/6. As the advance party of 1/6 was about to leave for the new CP, the Marine detachment from the *Newport News*, under the command of Captain John E Toth, arrived by helicopter. The detachment was sent ashore to search for a reported arms cache, and was attached to the advance party. After failing to turn up any arms or ammunition, members of the Marine guard were posted on the roof tops and in the upper floors of the university buildings to prevent snipers from firing down at the battalion CP. They remained in these positions until 6 May when they were helilifted back on board the *Newport News*.

The afternoon of 3 May, BLT 1/6's CP was in full operation with Company D and H&S Company occupying a perimeter defense bounded by Avenidas Alma Mater and Paulo III to the east and north, and Calles Nunez de Cacres and Aristides Faillo to the west and south. Company A screened from the north in a line stretching in the west from the juncture of Avenidas Abraham Lincoln and Pedro Henriquez Urena, east to the juncture of Avenidas Mexico and Maximo Gomez. Company C (less the 1st Platoon guarding the U.S. Embassy) was returned to 1/6's control that afternoon after having been under the opcon of 3/6 since 30 April. Upon detachment, the company moved by motor march from the polo field to an area approximately a half block west of Calle Tejada on Avenida George Washington where its CP was established. One platoon was detached and sent to the Hotel Hispaniola to provide security for the MEB CP. The remaining platoons conducted squad-sized vehicular patrols of the MSR.

Company B, the regimental reserve, was directed at 1915, on 4 May, to move into an assembly area at the polo field, prepared to move by trucks to blocking positions in the rear of BLT 3/6 where a rebel penetration was expected. When the penetration failed to materialize, the company was detached as the RLT reserve and returned to battalion control early the next morning. Back under battalion control, the company was given the western perimeter as its area of responsibility.

Early that same morning, upon orders from RLT-6, the 1st Battalion, 8th Marines was transported by helicopters from San Isidro into LZ-4 where it established its CP in the Belle Vista Golf House located next to the Embajador Hotel. For the next three days the battalion's and attached units' vehicles moved through the newly opened LOC with all the landing teams equipment and supplies.

That evening, BLT 1/8 received its operation order from RLT-6. The battalion was directed to provide security in its area of responsibility around the golf course and to provide one officer and 60 enlisted men for the security of the beach supply area (Red Beach) at Haina. Once in position, the battalion received sporadic sniper fire Company D conducted motorized patrols throughout the battalion area to prevent the rebels from moving in closer

The next few weeks saw little change in the situation as both battalions continued work in improving their positions. BLT 1/6 improved its checkpoints along the northern boundary of the ISZ. Company C, minus the one platoon at the MEB CP, was relocated to University City on 8 May, establishing defensive positions along the eastern portion of the battalion's boundary. The battalion was engaged during this period in providing security detachments to the AID building, and in protecting food and medical distribution points at the College of Santo Domingo and the Carol Morgan School until 21 May when the battalion began to be relieved by OAS forces.

Simultaneously with the deployment of Marine forces, units from the Army 82d AbnDiv were moved from Fort Bragg, North Carolina, to Pope AFB where they were flown to DomRep onboard C-130s. The 3d Brigade (2 Battalions), mentioned previously, arrived the evening of 30 April, followed by two battalions of the 2d Brigade on 3 May and two more battalions of the 2d Brigade on 3 May. The last major deployment of Army forces was completed on 4 May with the arrival of two battalions of the 1st Brigade. By the end of 4 May, there were 11,554 Army troops and 6,142 Marines in the objective area. Various supporting units continued to be deployed until 17 May when the peak build-up of U.S. forces was reached--14,889 Army, 7,958 Marines, and 1,001 Air Force Forces previously nominated but not required in DomRep were returned to DefCon 5 status.[50]

Section 6
Establishment of the U.S. Command, Dominican Republic[51]

With the deployment of Marine and Army units to DomRep, it was the desire of the JCS to establish at the appropriate time a command that would report directly to CinCLant Prior to the arrival of the 82d AbnDiv, no provisions had been made for a Joint Land Force Commander. This was temporarily corrected by designating General York at the commander of all Army and Marine forces ashore in DomRep.

It was the intention of CinCLant to designate General Palmer as Commander, U.S. Command, Dominican Republic (USComDomRep) as soon as positive control and communications were established among U.S. forces. Command interim arrangements were put into effect on 1 May by CinCLant. General Palmer was assigned control over those Army and Marine units that were under the command of General York, reporting as CTF-120 and Commander, Land Forces, DomRep., General Palmer was further directed to establish a joint air control coordination center for all air operations over, entering, and exiting DomRep. Those Army, Navy, and Air Force forces committed to POWER PACK that were not located in country remained under CinCARLant, CinCLantFlt, and CinCAFLant respectively General Palmer was authorized direct liaison with the other task force commanders (CTF-121 and CTF-124) to levy support requirements. Military operations, and civil affairs and psychological warfare operations were to be conducted in coordination with recognized Dominican military leaders and Ambassador Bennett respectively

Admiral Masterson still retained command of JTF-122 with the exception of those forces under General Palmer.

Admiral Masterson in a message to Vice Admiral Thomas H. Moorer (CinCLantFlt) indicated that General Palmer would soon be established ashore in his headquarters at the Trujillo Palace with adequate communications to assume command of all U.S. ground forces in DomRep In view of this, Admiral Masterson recommended the disestablishment of JTF-22 upon Palmer's assumption of the command. Since the naval task force was scheduled to revert to the operational control of CinCLantFlt, Admiral Masterson felt that the naval forces would be overstaffed with Admiral McCain (CTF-124) already in DomRep and Rear Admiral Reuben T. Whitaker (ComPhibGru-4) due to arrive on 7 May to assume command of the amphibious forces (CTF-128)

Accepting the recommendation made by Admiral Masterson on 6 May, CinCLant dissolved JTF-122 and TF-120 the next day and designated General Palmer as USComDomRep, effective at 1200, 7 May. All naval forces in DomRep were placed under the command of Admiral McCain, and he was designated CTF-124. General Bouker was designated as Commander, U.S Naval Forces, DomRep and Commander, Landing Forces (CTG-124.8) Admiral Masterson, on board the *Newport News*, departed the DomRep area that same afternoon for Norfolk.

CinCARLant, CinCLantFlt, and CinCAFLant were now responsible to ComUSDomRep for providing forces; controlling movement to and from DomRep, and logistical support The naval components would consist of U.S. Marines ashore, but would not include any of the ships. This command relationship remained until 29 May when Brazilian General Hugo Panesco Alvim arrived in DomRep and assumed command of the Inter-American Peace Force (IAPF) of which U S. Forces were a part. General Alvim's command included only the U.S. ground forces (Marines, Army, and Air Force); the naval units still remained under the command of Admiral McCain.

Section 7
Political Actions[52]

A great deal of criticism by the U.S. press has been levied against the Administration for not attempting to use the machinery available to the OAS for collective action in DomRep. What little OAS action there was before the Marines went ashore took place during that period when the National Police were unable to provide adequate protection to U.S. and foreign nationals. The decision to land Marines was made only after the police and military were no longer able to provide this protection. Not to have acted quickly would surely have brought about the loss of many lives.

It was on the initiative of the U.S. that the InterAmerican Peace Committee of the OAS was first called into session to discuss the situation in the DomRep. This meeting was called on 27 April, and from that time forward, the U.S. repeatedly attempted to conclude a peaceful settlement. On the 28th, the U.S. called for further discussion of the crisis. No action was taken by the OAS at this time as it was felt that the junta would be able to contain the rebel forces.[53]

That evening, as the situation in the DomRep deteriorated, the U S. requested a special session of the Council of the OAS It was concluded at this meeting that the Council was not empowered to act and that it was necessary to invoke the Rio Treaty or convene a meeting of the Consultation of Foreign Ministers (CFM). A 48-hour delay was requested in order to allow the members to consult with their home governments Because of the urgency, the U.S. was able to move the meeting up to the evening of 29 April. Convening at 2230, the meeting carried over into the early hours of the 30th The U.S. representative to the OAS, Ambassador Ellsworth Bunker, notified the Council at this time that the U S was reinforcing its military forces in the face of a lack of law and order and to protect not only U.S. and foreign nationals, but also to prevent excessive vandalism brought on by some of the Dominicans themselves.

Ambassador Bunker pointed out that U.S. action was not inconsistent with its inter-American obligations and that the U.S. was not intruding into the domestic affairs of the country, but simply assuming the obligation of saving lives in a situation where no authority existed to provide law and order. It was stressed that the U.S. had no candidate for leading the government of the DomRep, this was a matter for the Dominican people to decide for themselves. It was up to the OAS to find the means to assist the people in establishing a government which could meet the international obligations of the hemisphere In view of the above, Ambassador Bunker verbally requested the Council to issue an appeal for a cease-fire by both sides and concluded with a reading of the proposed resolution.

The cease-fire resolution passed at 0200 on 30 April called for an immediate end to hostilities and the establishment of an International Safety Zone (ISZ) which would include the U.S. and most of the other foreign Embassies.

That afternoon, the CFM, meeting in executive session, authorized the Secretary General, Dr Jose Mora of Uruguay, to go to DomRep to assist the Papal Nuncio (Monsignor Emanuele Clarizio) in his peace-making mission and "to indicate the presence of the OAS.": That afternoon during the meeting of the Council, a Mexican resolution calling for the establishment of a five-man Peace Committee to go to the DomRep to seek the re-establishment of peace and normal conditions was approved. This committee was composed of the OAS Ambassadors from Argentina, Brazil, Colombia, Guatemala, and Panama. Arriving in DomRep on 2 May, the members were amazed to find that they were unable to move between United States Army and Marine positions because of rebel sniping fire.

From the beginning of hostilities, the U.S. was continually working for a cease-fire. However, each and every effort to arrange for a cease-fire was frustrated by the hostile fire of the rebels. Because of these failures, Ambassador Bennett became increasingly distrustful of the rebels' intentions.

Partly as a result of this mistrust, President Johnson sent ex-Ambassador John Martin to DomRep on 30 April as his special envoy. Ambassador Martin was a political liberal with good connections among the various anti-Trujillo elements in Santo Domingo. He was also quite familiar with the Dominican Republic The White House idea was that Mr. Martin could take a fresh look at the Dominican situation and at the same time try to open new contacts with the rebels. As Ambassador to the Dominican Republic during the seven-month tenure of Bosch, Mr. Martin was held in high esteem by the former president, his associates, and a great many other Dominicans

The first cease-fire between the rebels and the junta was attempted by the U.S. on 30 April at a meeting attended by the junta, Ambassador Bennett, the Papal Nuncio acting for the rebels, and General York (Commanding General, 82d AbnDiv and Commander of all ground forces in DomRep) representing Admiral Masterson. The resulting cease-fire agreement signed at 1630 provided that: it would apply to all persons, regardless of ideology; that the OAS would be asked to provide a commission to arbitrate the present troubles; and a cease-fire would take effect that night at 2345 It soon became apparent that the rebels would only adhere to a cease-fire if it was to their advantage.

Ambassador Martin, together with the Papal Nuncio, visited Colonel Caamano at rebel headquarters on 1 May to work out the details of the cease-fire signed the previous day. Both sides during this meeting agreed to the boundaries of an International Safety Zone with the stipulation that U.S. forces would not move from their present positions When Ambassador Martin reported back to Ambassador Bennett, it was found that the ISZ negotiated by Martin did not conform with Admiral Masterson's recommendation nor was the change coordinated with him.

The northern boundary of the ISZ as originally proposed by Admiral Masterson ran from the juncture of Avenida San Martin and Avenida Presidenta Rios (Checkpoint D), southwest to the polo field, then south to the sea. The ISZ as negotiated by Martin ran from the juncture of Avenida Presidenta Rios and San Juan Bosco (Checkpoint C), southwest to the polo field, looping back to Avenida Abraham Lincoln and south to the sea.[54] This decision placed Checkpoints C and D in exposed positions General Tompkins, representing CJTF-122, objected in the strongest language (politely, of course) "that to have the military committed unilaterally to new boundaries and rules, and then fail to tell the military, was an unexcusable piece of madness and one that I took violent objection." (See Map 3)

No one was able to determine who had marked the map, all present disclaiming any part in the matter. Ambassador Martin offered to go back and re-negotiate the ISZ. This offer was turned down by General Tompkins as politically undesirable; he took the responsibility of accepting the agreement for CJTF-122, declaring that the Marine forces would be able to handle the agreement.

With the arrival of the OAS Peace Committee a formal truce agreement aimed at ending the civil war was signed on 5 May by the two contending forces; the rebel government that had ousted the Reid government and the military junta. The "Act of Santo Domingo" tasked the OAS with the supervision of the ceasefire. It provided for: (1) a cease-fire, as agreed to on 30 April; (2) the establishment of the ISZ; (3) an OAS guarantee for the protection and safety of all persons within the zone of refuge; (4) distribution of food, medical supplies, and hospital equipment supplied by the OAS; (5) medical and sanitary personnel to have free access to all parts of the city and other Dominican territory; (6) and a guaranty of the safety and evacuation of all persons who sought asylum in foreign embassies and diplomatic missions.

The breakdown of services in Santo Domingo had created many problems for the Dominican people. There were those who had not eaten for days, and a great need existed for medical supplies and attention for the sick and wounded The scores of dead bodies that had lain in the streets for days were creating a health hazard.

To assist in these problems initially, the JCS directed the movement of medical units to DomRep. Five medical emergency teams and 30,000 pounds of medical supplies were airlifted into DomRep on 1 May. The Assistant Secretary of State (desiguate) for Economic Affairs, Mr. A. Soloman, was sent to coordinate the relief effort to provide food, clothing, blankets, and medical supplies and personnel to the Dominican people. Ambassador Bunker, on 3 May, brought to the attention of the General Committee of the CFM the need for medical supplies, food, and assistance for the sick and wounded. A resolution was unanimously passed that day urgently appealing to the OAS members to send such food, medicines, doctors, and nurses to DomRep as they could.

The U.S. ship *Alcoa Ranger* was dispatched to DomRep carrying 80 tons of dry milk, 189,000 pounds of flour, 500,000 pounds of vegetable oil, and 1.6 million pounds of cornmeal. The distribution of food and medical supplies was accomplished through the Dominican Red Cross, Peace Corps volunteers, the 42d Civil Affairs Company, USA, and by the troops along the line of contact.

The U.S. Navy distributed 175 tents and the necessary medical supplies to the Dominican Red Cross for use as aid stations because of overcrowding of the civilian hospitals. In addition, a 60-bed Collecting and Clearing Hospital was transferred on 4 May from San Isidro to the area around the Embajador Hotel for civilian use. At this time, the only country other than the U.S. to contribute supplies to DomRep was Venezuela

By 6 May military hospitals were no longer needed as the Dominican hospitals could handle the load. U.S. forces continued, however, to furnish first aid at the aid stations and distribute food supplies along their defensive positions.

Fighting continued between the rebels and junta in spite of all actions taken by the OAS. President Johnson, on 16 May, sent a four-man fact-finding mission to DomRep. This group consisted of Presidential Assistant McGeorge Bundy, Under Secretary of Defense Cyrus R. Vance, Under Secretary of State for Economic Affairs Thomas C. Mann, and Under Secretary of State for Inter-American Affairs John H. Vaughn.

Their mission was to lend assistance to the OAS and to the people and leaders of the Dominican Republic to bring about the end of fighting, to establish a representative and democratic government, to eliminate the threat of Communist subversion, to facilitate the inclusion of U.S. forces in the Inter-American Force, and to provide for the progressive reduction and withdrawal of those forces not needed in DomRep

The collapse of the original group of rebels left the leadership in the hands of pro-Bosch, Communist, and extremist elements, armed by the original rebels, who carried on the fight. These elements roamed the city of Santo Domingo at will, terrorizing entire neighborhoods and indiscriminately firing their weapons. What had begun as a popular democratic revolution moved into the control of those who were believed to be Communist conspirators. As President Johnson stated over a nationwide radio-TV network on 2 May:

> The American nations cannot, must not,
> and will not permit the establishment of another
> Communist government in the Western Hemisphere

Ambassador Bunker stated the aims of the U.S. were to give assistance to the OAS and to the people and leaders of DomRep, to help bring an end to the fighting and bloodshed, to aid in the establishment of a broadly representative government based on democratic, constitutional principles, to eliminate the threat of present and future subversion of the government of DomRep by the establishment of a regime incompatible with the declared principles of the inter-American system, and to facilitate the progressive reduction and eventual withdrawal of foreign military forces in DomRep.[55] It was repeated many times over by U.S. officials that the U.S. supported no single man or any single group of men in DomRep. The only goal was to prevent any Communist takeover in the western hemisphere and to do this without further bloodshed.

Strict neutrality was much harder to achieve in view of the many political and military problems which beset the U.S. during the crisis. Even the establishment of the LOC, for example, providing a link-up between Army and Marine units contributed to this problem. The LOC served to isolate the rebel forces in the old city, keeping them from being reinforced by their counterparts in the north. Additionally when the junta forces of General Imbert Barreras began their attack on 13 May against rebel forces to the north, those rebels to the south were prevented by U.S Forces from going north, since Army and Marine units were under orders to keep both rebels and junta forces out of the LOC.

The U.S. news media took this opportunity to accuse the U S. of indirectly helping the junta forces. Later on, however, they failed to point up the contrary effect when the junta forces were not allowed to cross the LOC to attack those rebel forces to the south.

Further evidence of U.S. impartiality was the directive by USComDomRep ordering U S. forces to avoid actions indicating that the U.S. sided with any one faction and directing that no junta forces would be used in conjunction with any U.S. operations, roadblocks, blockades, or any defensive positions. Junta forces would only be used in a liaison capacity or as interpreters U.S. military forces were also forbidden to enter into any negotiations with the rebels.

Section 8
Stabilization[56]

The first cease-fire as negotiated on 30 April restricted U.S forces at a crucial moment when rebel forces had gained control of most of Cuidad Nueva (Old City) and when the regular Dominican forces had withdrawn in a demoralized state

To advance beyond those limits established by Ambassador Martin with the rebels could only be undertaken with the approval of the OAS. Initially this left the U.S. forces in a situation where full military power could not be exploited until a ground link was established between Marine and Army units. Situations of this nature continued until 17 May when the first Marine elements were sent back onboard ship to prepare for re-embarkation.

It became apparent several days after the initial landing that the U.S. Embassy was located too close to the eastern boundary of the Marine ISZ Movement in and around the Embassy grounds had become dangerous because of the sniper fire. To alleviate this situation, and with the sanction of the OAS, Company K was ordered, on 2 May, to move its defensive positions to a point two blocks east with its left flank at Avenida Mexico, then south along Calle Pedro A. Lluberes to Avenida Bolivar, west along Bolivar to Calle Sorocco Sanchez, and south along Sanchez to Calle Santiago, tying in with Company L. Once in position the company began receiving light small arms fire that continued throughout that day and night. Early the next morning as fire was received from the north along Calle Pedro Lluberes one Marine was killed. (See Map 3)

With the arrival of the OAS Peace Commission in Santo Domingo on 2 May, political considerations once again took precedence. After observing the situation, the Commission requested the U.S. to provide security to the Embassies of Equador and San Salvador. Two days later, Company L was ordered to advance four blocks east to Avenida Pasteur so as to place the embassies within the ISZ.[57] The move was completed that afternoon without opposition. As night defensive positions were being prepared, the company came under attack from five rebels moving west along Avenida George Washington. After a short fire fight the rebels withdrew, leaving three dead behind.

After the movement of Companies K and L was completed, Lieutenant Colonel Pederson directed the establishment of a modified people-to-people program. This program had the twofold objective of determining the attitude of the people towards the landing and occupation of the city by the Marines. The majority of the people indicated they were glad the Marines were there to stop the bloodshed which had been as prevalent during the early days. A more practical reason given was the protection of their homes and property by the Marines. The areas occupied by Companies K and L were in the middle class districts and these people were generally better off than in Company I's area which bordered the middle and lower class districts. The people in the lower class districts were not in as good circumstances and in many cases desperately in need of food that was supplied by the Marines. With few exceptions the people were glad the Marines were there during the early days. This attitude changed as the threat of violence by the rebels subsided.

With easing of tensions, thought was given to planning for future contingencies General Bouker, on 3 May, was advised by the Commanding General, FMFLant to unload only those items of equipment and supplies essential to the mission and to maintain a high degree of readiness to deploy on short notice for full scale combat in another area. To achieve these ends the LSU was redesignated as the LSG on 4 May, bringing the issuance of supplies and equipment under centralized control. Tasked organized under the MEB, all Class I, II, IV, and V supplies were to be distributed from the primary LSA located at the landing zone next to the Embajador Hotel. Second echelon maintenance continued to be performed at the BSA at the port of Haina.

As the situation stabilized, General Palmer decided, on 5 May, to land the reserve battalion lying offshore When preparations were underway to land the 1st Battalion, 2d Marines, Admiral McCain requested the landing be deferred until the next day. After a conference by the two commanders, the decision was made to cancel the landing because of CinCLant's responsibility to meet any contingency that might arise in the Caribbean area With the original Carib Ready Force (BLT 3/6) already ashore, BLT 1/2, in addition to being tasked as the floating reserve, was also the interim Carib Ready Force.

Another determining factor taken into consideration was the fact that the 1st Battalion, 2d Marines had only recently returned from a Mediterranean deployment and was scheduled for a reorganization of personnel on 1 June. HMM-263, also afloat with the battalion, was scheduled for deployment to the Western Pacific on 1 October. For the squadron to be in place by that date, the leaves, travel, and movement phase had to begin by 1 June Since these two units were uncommitted they would be in the best position to return to the States at the earliest possible moment.

To consolidate the Marine units, Colonel Daughtry shifted his command post ashore on 4 May where it was co-established with the MEB at the Hispaniola Hotel. The 2d Battalion, 10th Marines which had departed Morehead City by ship on 2 May landed its units (Hqdrs and F Battery) over Red Beach, 8-9 May, where they joined E Battery and the Howtar Battery, 3d Battalion, 10th Marines. E Battery had landed previously with the 6th MEU. The Howtar Battery was airlifted into San Isidro on 3 May. In order to maximize the capabilities of all the available artillery these units were consolidated into Battery Group Echo on 10 May. Lieutenant Colonel Kenneth C. Williams assumed command of the group, establishing his command post in the vicinity of the Embajador Hotel The group was tasked with the missions of providing support to the scheme of maneuver of RLT-6 and the firing of counterbattery fire.

Several instances of U.S. forces straying into rebel territory occurred during the second week of the landings. Shortly after 0830 on 6 May, two vehicles from the Howtar Battery departed the ISZ, en route to the San Isidro airfield for supplies. A few minutes after leaving the perimeter, they made a wrong turn in the corridor. Driving into rebel territory, near Independencia Park, they ran into rebel fire from automatic weapons which killed one Marine and wounded two others. The four remaining Marines were listed as missing until later that day when two were returned from rebel territory. Earlier that morning, Mr. Satin, a peace corpsman, had made arrangements to meet with Hector Aristy, a member of the rebels, to discuss procedures for food distribution. Unaware of the earlier action between the Marines and rebels, Mr. Satin found the two captured Marines upon his arrival at rebel headquarters. Immediately, Satin contacted Aristy and obtained the release of the Marines. The two remaining missing Marines were found to be dead when Dominican civilians returned the bodies late that afternoon at the Embajador Hotel. The Army was faced with a similar occurrence the same day when four soldiers strayed into rebel territory. Abandoning their M-37 truck, they managed to make their way to 3/6 lines.

Rebel activity was responsible for some casualties incurred by U.S. civilians on 6 May. A reporter and photographer from the *Miami Herald* during that same morning were wounded by Marine fire as they were returning to Company I's lines. It appeared that the Dominican driver of the car carrying the newsmen panicked and threw the car in reverse just as the rebels began firing at the Marine positions across no-man's-land. As the Marines replied in kind, the car was caught in the crossfire Both newsmen were immediately evacuated to the *Boxer* for medical treatment when it was determined who they were

As the air threat lessened in DomRep, preparations were begun during the early part of May to return the operational control of the two fixed-winged squadrons to the 2d MAW. VMFA-323 returned from Roosevelt Roads on 8 May in order that personnel transfers could be effected and the unit could prepare for its scheduled deployment to WestPac in October. VMF(AW)-451 followed at the end of the month and was placed under the operational control of Carrier Air Wing 8 for carrier requalification training prior to its deployment to the Mediterranean on 24 August.

The 3d Battalion, 6th Marines was ordered relieved by the 1st Battalion, 8th Marines on 9 May. In preparation, the relieving force sent an advance party of officers to 3/6's positions the night before to acquaint them with the area they were about to occupy. At 0600 the next morning, a final briefing was conducted for company commanders and staff members of both battalions. The relief was planned to phase one platoon into one company at a time. This method was decided upon as the best way of denying the rebels knowledge of such a move at a vulnerable time and to avoid signs that a relief by fresh troops was being effected. There was a fear that this would alarm the rebels into some form of retaliation The relief began at 0820, proceeded smoothly and with dispatch, and was completed at 1325. No rebel activity was reported during the move.

After moving into its new positions, 1/8 was directed to straighten the eastern boundary along Phase line CAIRO. Operation FORWARD MARCH was put into effect on 12 May Completed late that afternoon, the battalion front now formed a continuous line from the juncture of Avenida Francis and Calle Rosa Duarte, south along Avenida Pasteur to the sea. Several checkpoints were established on the streets leading in and out of the ISZ. The battalion now assumed the responsibility for providing security to the American Embassy. (See Map 3)

The 3d Battalion, 6th Marines after deploying to the west, occupied new positions encompassing the Embajador Hotel, polo fields, and a portion of the golf course including the club house which became the battalion CP. Company L was tasked with providing security for Red Beach at Haina and the CARE warehouse located at the fairgrounds, and for keeping the MSR open from Red Beach to LZ-4. The Guatemalan Ambassador requested that security be provided for his Embassy, which was furnished by the reconnaissance and 81mm mortar platoons. Sharing the perimeter defense were Battery F, 10th Marines and elements of the Landing Support Group. Throughout the next several days, the battalion busied itself with the improvement of existing positions and the construction of new positions. On 10 May, it became necessary to reduce the perimeter since the battalion had only three instead of four rifle companies for defense.

Plans were now prepared for the withdrawal of Marine forces with the easing of tensions The Commanding General, 2d Marine Division recommended that the withdrawal of its forces should be in the following order: (1) BLT 1/2; (2) BLT 1/8; (3) BLT 1/6; (4) 4th MEB and supporting headquarters, and (5) BLT 3/6 at which time it would resume the status as the Carib Ready Force [58]

With the consolidation of U.S positions being completed, General Palmer advised CinCLant, on 13 May, that the time had now come to seize the main rebel radio station, a source of bitter anti-American propaganda. This was concurred in by Ambassador Bennett The plan was never put into effect as the Government of National Reconstruction (GNR) mounted their offensive at this time and captured the radio station on 19 May. By 22 May, the GNR forces had swept and secured the area north of the LOC, leaving the National Palace--held by GNR forces and surrounded by rebel-held territory--as the only remaining position of direct contact between GNR and rebel forces.[59]

Section 9
Inter-American Peace Force[60]

At the tenth meeting of the Consultation of the Ministers of Foreign Affairs of the American Republics, which convened on 1 May, U S. Ambassador Ellsworth Bunker made first mention of an Inter-American Force Ambassador Bunker stated.

.   that my government regrets that there was no inter-American force available to respond to the needs of the people of the Dominican Republic and for the protection of the lives and safety of other nationals. My government would welcome the constitution of such a force as soon as possible. . . ."[61]

The landing of additional troops was reported to the Third Session of the General Assembly by Ambassador Bunker on 3 May. This was found to be necessary in order that adequate protection could be provided to the ISZ and IOC. In addition there was an estimated 5,000 U.S. and foreign nationals still awaiting evacuation.

The Papal Nuncio welcomed the action taken by the U.S. when he stated:

. . . I want to express my personnel gratitude to President Johnson for the humane contribution and for the protection of the foreign Embassies as well as the contribution to a cease-fire and the saving of human lives within the terms of OAS appeal. . . ."[62]

The Secretary General of the OAS, Dr. Jose A. Mora, together with several of the foreign ambassadors in the Dominican Republic, expressed essentially the same sentiments.

Ambassador Bunker, at the same session, presented to the Council a resolution for the creation of a multilateral inter--American force to assist the Five-man Peace Commission in putting to an end the tragic civil war in DomRep. This resolution was intended to make it possible for the American governments to contribute in meeting the emergency and to promote the establishment of democratic institutions in DomRep, a basic goal of the OAS. The resolution contained the necessary measures to organize and carry out this joint hemispheric venture and pointing out that U.S wished to withdraw its forces at the earliest time. Discussions concerning the creation of the multilateral forces continued until 6 May when the resolution was approved by the required minimum of 14 votes.

The resolution establishing the Inter-American Force (IAF)[63] provided for member states, who were willing and capable, to make contingents of their land, naval, air, or police forces available to the OAS in forming the IAF. This force was to cooperate in restoring normal conditions in the Dominican Republic, in maintaining the security and the inviolability of human rights to its inhabitants, and the establishment of an atmosphere of peace and conciliation permitting the functioning of democratic institutions The commanders of each contingent were·to work out directly among themselves and with the OAS a unified command for the coordinated and effective composition of this Force. The OAS Unified Command would assume full responsibility for the purposes contained in the resolution at such time as adequate forces became available. Measures for the withdrawal of the IAF from the Dominican Republic would be determined by the OAS. This was construed to mean that time when democratic order was established.

Supporting the resolution were the United States, Dominican Republic, Argentina, Bolivia, Brazil, Colombia, Guatemala, Costa Rica, Nicaragua, Panama, El Salvador, Honduras, Haiti, and Paraguay. Opposed were Mexico, Uruguay, Chile, Ecuador, and Peru. Venezuela abstained because it disagreed with the wording of the resolution, but the Caracas delegate approved of its substance, announcing they would supply troops. Other members that promised to send troops were Guatemala, Brazil, Costa Rica, Honduras, and Paraguay.

This opened a new phase in the DomRep operations and a new course in the relationships between the members of the OAS. In preparation for the possible establishment of the Inter-American Force, the Joint Chiefs of Staff undertook studies relating to force contributions by OAS member nations and command structures. Plans were made for the bulk of the logistic requirement to come from U.S. sources. In reply to a request by the OAS Commission, the Inter-American Defense Board (IADB) also studied the formation of the IAF and made recommendations to the Commission along lines similar to those of the JCS. An IADB military liaison group was appointed to facilitate contact between the IADB and the Commission.

Another resolution approved on 22 May by the Council of Foreign Ministers establishing the IAF as a peace-keeping force and was essentially the same as the one passed on 6 May with one exception. The ministers requested the Government of Brazil to designate the Commander of the Inter-American Peace Force and the United States to designate the Deputy Commander.

Following the signing of the 22 May resolution, Secretary General Mora, stated:

The purpose of the IAPF is clearly not one of intervention, but rather one of rendering assistance to the people of a sister nation . . . that the objectives for which the IAPF was created fall within those broad provisions of the Charter which are concerned with matters affecting the peace and security of the Western Hemisphere. Peace, prosperity and justice are indivisible and interdependent. Where these are lacking in one nation, it must be a matter of concern to all . . .
[64]

Operation PRESS AHEAD, the deployment of the IAPF, began with the arrival, on 14 May, of a 250-man Honduran rifle company. This was followed by other IAPF forces so that by 29 May the force, less U S. units, consisted of: the Honduran unit; a Costa Rican Civil Guard detachment (21 men); a medical team from El Salvador (3 men), a Nicaraguan rifle company (164 men); and a Brazilian infantry battalion (1,129 men), which included a company of Brazilian

Marines. During June and July, Paraguay sent a rifle company and a communications platoon of 213 men. Earlier, on 7 May, two Venezuelan destroyers had arrived in San Juan with instructions to report to the Commander IAPF. However, prior to actually reporting, they were directed by their government to return to their home station.

The IAPF was formally established on 23 May, and six days later the designated IAPF Commander, Brazilian General Alvim arrived in Santo Domingo and assumed command with General Palmer as his deputy

The 4th MEB was directed on 20 May to bivouac the Honduran and Nicaraguan rifle companies in its area, locating these units at the intersection of Calle Roma and Avenida Bolivar. Three days later, the 22-man Brazilian advance party joined these units in the same area. Members of the MEB staff held a briefing on 31 May to acquaint the OAS forces with the tactical situation in preparation for their assuming the responsibility of the ISZ. The relief of U.S. forces began on 2 June with the Brazilian force occupying the National Palace. Five days later the Latin Brigade of the IAPF relieved elements of the 82d AbnDiv in the eastern portion of the ISZ. This demonstrated the capacity of the OAS to adjust to new conditions and to deal with new problems, problems perhaps not foreseen at the time of the writing of the OAS Charter.

Section 10
Withdrawal[65]

The resolution establishing the Inter-American Peace Force laid the groundwork for the withdrawal of U.S forces from DomRep. This was in keeping with paragraph four of the resolution calling for the transformation of forces in DomRep into a force that would not be of one state or a group of states, but that of the OAS seeking to bring about the restoration of normal conditions in DomRep Ambassador Bunker reported to the Ministers of Foreign Affairs of the American Republics, on 6 May, that at such time as the Inter-American Peace Force was in a position to provide for law and order in the DomRep, U.S. forces not needed as part of the IAPF would be withdrawn.[66]

CinCLant, two days later, submitted his views on force requirements and suggested an order of withdrawal of U.S. forces to the JCS, based on recommendations from General Palmer In the interest of overall readiness in the Caribbean area, it was found most desirable to withdraw the Marines as soon as it was both militarily and politically feasible. This decision was based on the need to reconstitute the Carib Ready Force and to make ready the back-up forces of the Fleet Marine Force and their amphibious ships. CinCLant would find it easier to meet any contingency that might arise in the Mediterranean as well as the Caribbean with the withdrawal of the Marine units first.[67]

The U S. Ambassador to Santo Domingo advised Secretary of State Rusk on 22 May that BLT 1/2, already afloat, would be withdrawn immediately for employment elsewhere. He also advised that a second BLT could be withdrawn, at least to ships offshore, with the arrival of the 1,200-man Brazilian contingent [68] This was in keeping with Ambassador Bunker's 26 May announcement to the OAS that the U.S. would withdraw 1,700 troops from its forces in DomRep.

CinCLant, on 25 May, submitted his recommendation to the JCS for the withdrawal of U.S. forces with the arrival of the various Latin American contingents His decision was based on the assumption that the political situation would be stabilized and the IAPF would be capable of assisting the Dominican National Police and military forces in maintaining law and order

General Palmer recommended that BLT 1/2 and HMM-263, onboard the *Okinawa*, be withdrawn initially, followed by Headquarters, 6th MEU and BLT 3/6 which would be reconstituted as the Carib Ready Force. In addition, miscellaneous army support units no longer required could also leave at this time. On Withdrawal Day plus 6, the two remaining Marine BLTs (1/8 and 1/6) and Headquarters, 4th MEB could depart by amphibious shipping, followed seven days later by two airborne infantry battalions together with their reinforcing units. The U.S contribution to the IAPF was visualized as consisting of four airborne infantry battalions plus their appropriate headquarters and reinforcing units, including an air assault helicopter company. All logistical support forces were to remain ashore in DomRep where they would provide support to the IAPF. Two of the remaining airborne infantry battalions were to maintain a quick-reaction capability.

The JCS directed the withdrawal of BLT 1/2 and HMM-263 on 26 May. Departing that same evening, minus the battalion's supporting units, BLT 1/2 arrived at Onslow Beach on 29 May where it was helilifted ashore, reverting to the control of the 2d Marine Division. BLT 3/6 was ordered to re-embark on board the *Boxer* on 26 May. BLT 1/6 began evacuating its positions around University City during the early morning hours of the 26th, completing the relief of 3/6 by 0900 the same morning.

The re-embarkation orders called for the phasing out of the 3d Battalion, 6th Marines, with the troops loading onboard the *Boxer* first by helo from LZ-4. Bulk cargo and attachments were moved to Haina where they were back loaded over Red Beach to other ships of the squadron. After completing loading on the 31st, ships of TG 44.9 steamed to a ready position fifty miles west of Santo Domingo

Various Marine supporting units not required in DomRep were loaded aboard the *La Salle* and departed the area, arriving at Morehead City, North

Carolina, on 31 May, where they were returned to 2d Marine Division operational control.[69]

. . On 30 May, ProvMag-60, together with HMM-264, reembarked all personnel and equipment on board the *Boxer*. The helicopter squadron continued supporting the MEB until 8 June when the Task Group departed the area and was returned to its normal status of being ready to react within 72 hours within its area of responsibility.

The participation of Marine aviation in the DomRep crisis once again proved an important factor in providing support to forces ashore. The landing of assault troops and the evacuation of civilians during the early days of the operation, without the loss of a single life, clearly demonstrated the skill of the pilots. Close air support, while its use was never required, was ever present, ready to support the ground forces if the need arose.

Commander, Caribbean Sea Frontier (ComCaribSeaFron), on 27 April, alerted VMFA-323 to prepare four aircraft for possible missions over the DomRep. For the next two days the squadron was placed on a 30-minute ground alert for use as a show of force and support of the naval forces in and around the Dominican Republic. From 29 April until 1 May, VMFA-323 maintained a combat air patrol (CAP) during daylight hours over the Ready Group. That same day the squadron was placed under the operational control of the 6th MEU, subsequently assumed by ProvMag-60 the next day. Until relieved on 8 May, VMFA-323 flew 166 sorties (26 combat air patrols and 140 low-level reconnaissance flights) for a total of 345 flight hours during its 10-day participation in Operation POWER PACK.

VMFA(AW)-451 was deployed to Roosevelt Roads, Puerto Rico, and tasked with the same mission as VMFA-323. The squadron was placed under the opcon of the 6th MEU upon its arrival in Roosevelt Roads on 1 May. Transferred to ProvMag-60 the next day, the squadron flew combat air patrols over the Task Force, and road and beach reconnaissance missions over the objective area. A photo reconnaissance aircraft (RF8A) of VMCJ-2 attached to VMFA-451, was pursued by a Dominican Air Force F-51 during the morning of 14 May while on a photo mission. To provide protection, the squadron was given the added mission of providing armed escorts to future photo reconnaissance missions. Later that month, the squadron was relieved and returned to its parent organization. VMFA-451 had conducted a total of 387 sorties (232 combat air patrols, 34 photo escorts, 115 road, and 6 beach reconnaissance missions) for a total of 726 flying hours.

The real work-horses of Marine aviation in DomRep proved to be the two helicopter squadrons, HMM-263 and -264, with HMM-264 being first on the scene as the contingency squadron of Carib 2-65. From 27 April to 28 June,

this squadron participated not only in the DomRep operation, but also in three training exercises as part of the Ready Force. The early days of the crisis saw the squadron conducting the first tactical night vertical assault into an unsecured landing zone under combat conditions The landing was further complicated by bad weather and sporadic small arms fire in the landing zone. In addition to helo-lifting BLT 3/6 ashore, a total of 2,159 civilian men, women, and children were evacuated to U.S. ships off shore without incurring any accidents or injuries. The professional ability of the officers and men was pointed up by the fact that during this time the squadron celebrated its 50,000th accident
--free flight hour. The squadron during its three month deployment as the contingency squadron flew a total of 6,031 sorties and carried 19,140 troops, 2,159 civilians, and 1,293 tons of supplies, for a total of 5,329 flight hours.

Arriving in DomRep on board the *Okinawa* on 4 May, HMM-263 also amassed an impressive record. Placed in the multi-role of supporting U.S. forces ashore as well as being tasked as the interim contingency squadron for the Caribbean area, HMM-263 conducted 657 sorties and carried 1,361 passengers and 120,000 pounds of supplies for a total flight time of 827 hours.

The final withdrawal of Marine units began on 2 June. The 1st Battalion, 8th Marines was relieved in place by the 1st Battalion, 325th Airborne Infantry and 1/8 moved by truck to Red Beach, embarking on board the APA *Monrovia* Supplies and equipment were loaded the next day, and the ship departed the area for Morehead City. Arriving on 6 June, the battalion began transporting personnel and equipment to Camp Lejeune, completing the move by the next afternoon

On the afternoon of 3 June, as the 2d Battalion, 325th Airborne Infantry conducted a reconnaissance of the battalion's area, final arrangements were made to relieve BLT 1/6. The Army units began arriving at 0800 and by that afternoon the relief had been completed. At 1800, troops and equipment started loading onboard the APA *Chilton* and AKA *Capricornus* from Red Beach at the port of Haina Loading was completed on 5 June with the ships sailing for Morehead City, where they arrived on 9 June Debarkation and movement to Camp Lejeune was accomplished the same day

At the same time BLT 1/6 was loading, the 4th MEB, relieved of all tactical responsibilities, embarked part of its personnel onboard surface craft and the rest onboard aircraft for the move to Camp Lejeune. The 4th MEB, arriving back at Camp Lejeune, opened its CP at 2200 on 6 May.

Looking back at the operation, the first days were the roughest. The Marines found themselves frequently caught in the middle of two warring factions. Stray rounds and ricochets were more dangerous than direct fire. Sniper fire was sporadic and, fortunately, generally erratic and inaccurate. The snipers themselves were untrained youths whose unfamiliarity with their weapons rendered them dangerous irritants rather than effective opponents.

The checkpoints and roadblocks, operating on a 24-hour basis, were used to monitor all foot and vehicular traffic moving in and out of the ISZ. No restrictions were placed upon anyone moving in either direction provided they had a valid ID card issued by the national police. All males and vehicles were subject to search and anyone in possession of a weapon was detained and sent back to LZ-4 for interrogation. Any person whose name was on the Black or Gray list was also detained. These lists, containing the names of known Communists or Communist sympathizers were compiled by both U S and Dominican intelligence agencies and furnished the American forces. The troops manning the roadblocks and checkpoints became centers of attention to the native population. It was not long before they acquired the additional duties of food distribution points and medical treatment centers.

Santo Domingo presented an unusual contrast of war and peace. Battle-ready units were found bivouacked on the front yards and patios of expensive homes. Civilian traffic found its intersections blocked with tanks, Ontos, and mechanical mules mounting 106-mm recoilless rifles. Street vendors could be seen selling their wares to troops while shoeshine boys shined the shoes of combat-ready Marines. Occasional sniper fire brought instant reaction from the Marines who immediately cleared the streets of women and children before searching out and eliminating the offending sniper.

A guarded relaxation became possible as conditions began to return to normal, and the Marines could avail themselves of some of the niceties of civilian life on this vacation-type island. A swimming beach a few miles east of the city was used for recreation breaks. Ice suddenly appeared back on the scene to add a refreshing zest to the products of the local bottling plants. The days in Santo Domingo, hot and humid as they were, were modified by the ocean breeze. The nights were balmy, encouraging sound restful sleep in a plush Caribbean setting.

Yet, underlying it all was that sobering reminder of the basic seriousness of the campaign; the casualty reports. The majority of the casualties were received during the first week of the landing; the last was suffered on 18 May. Nine Marines were killed (4 in BLT 3/6, 1 in BLT 1/6, 2 in BLT 2/10, 1 in the 2d Service Battalion, and 1 in the 2d Engineer Battalion) while 30 were wounded (19 in BLT 3/6, 4 in BLT 1/8, 3 in 2/10, 1 in VMO-1, 2 in the 2d Engineer Battalion, and 1 in Headquarters, 6th Marines).

Section 11
Lessons Learned[70]

The overall objective of deploying U S. forces to the Dominican Republic was to maintain some degree of control over a completely disorganized urban society in order to bring about a political solution acceptable to the United States. To achieve this objective, operations were conducted in such a way that the U.S. retained the capability to control the outcome. However, this method of control, as understood in the traditional sense, was modified by the inclusion of political considerations requiring close civilian and military control at the highest levels of government in Washington.

The DomRep contingency plan proved conclusively that the U.S could respond rapidly to any contingency that might arise in the Caribbean area However, it was evident that certain modifications were necessary to make the plan more workable. The military found that in a state of political fluidity, improvisation was the better guide in arriving at a solution than rigid, prepared actions. This had the effect of providing measured responses in a variety of situations:

The Commander's Situation Report proved to be inadequate in providing detailed information on troop strength, equipment, deployment schedules, locations of units, intelligence, and other aspects of the operation. The time lag between the occurrence of events and the submission of the reports to the National Military Command Center was too great, although the reports themselves were sufficient in detail. This time lag resulted in placing many requests on field commanders which could have been alleviated by the use of supplementary reports for developing actions.

Command relationships proved sound for effective command and control. It became apparent early in the operation that coordination of plans, operations, and logistic support could be accomplished more quickly with the activation of component commands as soon as it appeared that joint action would be required. The deployment of Marine and Army airlifted units to DomRep might have been accomplished more efficiently had these units been activated earlier. The decision to conduct a night landing of the airborne units after they had been rigged for an airdrop deprived these units initially of vital combat equipment in a potentially dangerous situation. This graphically pointed out the need for timely warning and execution orders so that arrangements could be made for the early arrival of airfield control groups, aircraft control specialists, and materials handling equipment. This would have permitted more efficient and economical use of resources.

Army and Marine forces experienced the same problems upon landing at the San Isidro airfield. An average of 242 sorties were made and 1,946 tons of cargo were landed daily from 30 April-6 May. There were peak periods when 50 or more aircraft were arriving virtually together and slack periods when only two-three aircraft landed every two to three hours. Speed became essential at peak landing periods in clearing the taxiway of supplies and equipment to make room for the other incoming flights. This created the need for establishing staging areas where material could be segregated by category by the accepting unit

Marine techniques did not adequately cope with this problem as preliminary planning did not envision the need for coordination, control personnel, and equipment at the airfield. Once the need was recognized, it was not until 4 May that control and staging personnel from Marine Wing Service Group 27 and the 2d Force Service Regiment arrived on the scene. Personnel from BLTs 1/6 and 1/8 meanwhile had to stage their supplies manually, losing valuable time when palletized material had to be broken up for easier handling

The size and composition of the 6th MEU as foreseen in the Caribbean Contingency Plan was adequate. With the arrival and assumption of command by the 4th MEB, many of the supporting units experienced difficulty in performing their missions due to the increased workload and lack of trained personnel. This was particularly true in the air and logistic support units.

ProvMag-60, as long as it was operating with one helicopter squadron in support of one BLT, experienced no problems. As additional helicopter and fixed-wing squadrons were attached, serious personnel shortages appeared. Various members of the headquarters staff had to be detached to support the multiple operations at lower levels. These individuals had no backup replacements when their work ran on for extended periods. The commanding officer of the ProvMag was required to perform many of the special and executive staff functions personally, because of the lack of officers, cutting down on the time needed for other tasks required of a commanding officer.

The efficiency of the LSG suffered from lack of directive staff. The stripping of personnel from infantry units to assist in maintenance and processing of supplies not only decreased the capabilities of those units but placed inexperienced persons at the various supply and maintenance points. The problems of the LSG was further increased when the 4th MEB embarkation officer was not used in loading out the supplies and equipment. In many cases the officer who did the loading was left behind, leaving no one familiar with the loads available upon their arrival. This caused a great deal of time to be expended in determining what supplies were on hand.

Communications took on added importance with close control being exerted from Washington. Adequate communications were not available until Admiral Masterson, on board the *Newport News*, arrived in the area. Prior to the landing of the Marines from the Ready Force, the only link between the U S. Embassy and the United States was through commercial telephone and telegraph exchanges held by the rebel forces. Communications between the Ready Force and the U.S Embassy during the first few days of the landing was conducted by one of the Embassy officials who was an amateur radio operator. This lack of communications ashore prevented an early activation of USComDomRep.

Plans for the future call for the establishment of a three-way direct, reliable, and secure communication link between Washington-Embassy-on-the-scene commander This would provide an immediate coordination of in-country operations.

Units of the MEB experienced difficulties in using the Central Control AN/TSC-15 equipment of the FMF Mobile Command circuit. Communications personnel were unable to tune to the Naval Communications Station San Juan since the TSC-15 could only be tuned in one kilocycle increments. This required personnel at the Navy station to tune their equipment to the Marine unit. Recommendations were made that in the future, communication personnel should be trained to use receiver equipment that cannot be variably tuned and to preposition, in centrally located areas, the necessary communications equipment needed to maintain contact with Washington. It was noted that batteries B-451, switchboard SB-86, and teletypewriter TT-247 failed to stand up in bad weather, and rough handling Modifications to correct these deficiencies were submitted to the appropriate agencies.

Intelligence assumed a more complex role as a requirement for virtually all aspects of urban life in addition to traditional military intelligence. In many cases, the information was available within the Defense Intelligence Agency but not immediately available to the forces in DomRep because they were not on the standard distribution lists Actually, a great deal of information was available on DomRep, in fact, more than existed for many of the other Latin American countries. In operations having political overtones, information concerning public services and their locations, street numbering systems, communication facilities, political factions, military (both rebel and loyal) strengths, and maps of the area take on added importance.

A need for the activation of a CritiComm terminal to provide the MEB with special intelligence was realized early in the operation. Since the contingency plan did not call for this capability in the objective area, additional personnel and equipment had to be deployed to DomRep to establish a circuit for the exclusive use of the MEB.

While no serious logistical support problems were encountered, the handicap of utilizing one airfield and the lack of materials handling equipment imposed certain limitations in unloading incoming aircraft. The phasing in of logistical personnel and equipment of all U.S. forces into the area lagged excessively behind the arrival of combat and medical units This pointed out the need to provide for early arrival of logistical support and for contingency plans and operations to reflect realistically the limitating factors.

The deployment from CONUS of the seaborne elements of the 4th MEB was accomplished in a minimum of time on a crash basis Many of the smaller units of the incrementally deployed BLTs were without adequate stocks, and demands made upon the mountout stocks were not characteristic of the requirements of actual combat. It was apparent that plans have to be made to see that such required materials will be available in the future

The most critical item of supply during the early days of the landing was POL. This continued until 5 May when negotiations were concluded enabling U.S. forces to purchase POL from the commercial tank facilities located in Santo Domingo. Without these POL facilities in the area, the forces would have had to rely upon the Marine Bulk Fuel System which arrived in the area on board the LST 1178 on 5 May. This system could have been made available to all services for a short period of time without adverse effect on the requirements of the 4th MEB. Over a long period, however, POL would have been critical.

With the main thrust of the U.S. effort in DomRep in the political-economic-sociological fields, civil affairs and psychological warfare operations took on added importance USIA was given the responsibility for the overall coordination of psychological warfare operations. In a primarily political situation, as was the case in the DomRep, there is a great need for political and governmental training by key psychological warfare personnel and more in-depth comprehension of the psychological aspects by persons of all U.S. agencies.

It was determined that psychological warfare operations should begin as early as possible, and the plans should include qualified and properly trained people with adequate equipment prepared for deployment on minimum notice. In areas where English is not the spoken language, more emphasis should be placed on language qualification and the use of indigenous persons as a means of communication.

The mission of hastening the self-sufficiency of local government agencies and organizations by assisting in the restoration of the major functions of government, i e., public safety, health, welfare, education, public works, utilities, and economics was the overall responsibility of the Army's 42d Civil Affairs Company. It was a monumental task for such a small organization.

Both the civil affairs and psychological warfare staff of the military forces were unable to function at maximum capability because State/AID officials did not understand the capabilities of those units. It became evident that commanders of unified commands needed to place more emphasis at country and regional levels for more coordination between military and civilian agencies to enhance mutual understanding of civil affairs and psychological warfare requirement.

The need for a permanent civil affairs and psychological warfare staff with school-trained Marine personnel became apparent during the early days. While Army units, in addition to the 42d Civil Affairs Company, had a complete : G-5 section at corps and division headquarters, the 4th MEB had one legal officer in the G-1 section filling the billet of the civil affairs officer. An Army civil affairs officer was requested and supplied Fortunately this officer had participated in QUICK KICK VII with the MEB staff and was well acquainted with Marine procedures Since Marine units were located mainly in the middle-class areas, there were fewer problems encountered than in the lower--class areas occupied by the Army

A permanent civil affairs and psychological warfare staff would have been able to foresee some of the difficulties which occurred within their areas. Such problems as the distribution of food to the Dominican people, which was supposed to have received favorable reaction from the people, created bad feelings when the people outside of the city failed to receive any food. The rebels were able to use this against the U.S. forces in sowing seeds of discontent. Trained personnel would have been able to establish sufficient distribution points, plan for sufficient supplies, and counter any propaganda effort against the U.S

The U.S. news media played an important role in explaining to the world the reason for intervention in the DomRep by the United States. In many cases, however, the news was slanted and brought discredit to the United States when irresponsible news representatives gave great credibility to the propaganda efforts of the rebels. This greatly aided the anti-American propaganda efforts of the Communistic world. In order to keep this from happening in the future and to promote a more positive public affairs approach, it was felt by the military that the major U.S. news agencies should be alerted at the first sign of a troop deployment. This would have the effect of placing responsible newsmen on the scene of any overseas crisis within a matter of hours with the necessary logistical support to facilitate the immediate release of news.

Political considerations remained until the end of the operation a significant feature of U.S. policy. The announcement by the President of the withdrawal of specific numbers of personnel, not units, from DomRep forced Marine and Army units to phase out their forces in increments, which broke up their tactical unity. The consequence of this action resulted in leaving major units in a disorganized state, unavailable for immediate deployment elsewhere if the need arose.

Section 12
Conclusions

The initial dispatch of military forces to the Dominican Republic by the United States was purely and solely to provide protection to U.S. citizens. The landing of U.S. Marines stopped the needless bloodshed within the ISZ, which had taken the lives of many Dominicans, and the firing on U.S. and foreign nationals assembled at the Embajador Hotel. When the new and ominous threat of a Communist take-over began to emerge, U.S. military forces assumed the additional mission of preventing the establishment of another Communist state in the Western Hemisphere.

The DomRep operation brought to light four salient lessons, all of which will have to be considered in future contingency planning.

The first lesson is that care should be exercised in reaching any conclusions concerning amphibious and airborne capabilities   Since the deployment of Marine and Army units was conducted without opposition, careful consideration must be given to the shortcomings which occurred in command, communications, logistics, and the use of air in the operation. What little opposition that was encountered occurred when U.S. forces were first established ashore and deployed to accomplish U.S. objectives

The second lesson is the fact that this was not primarily a military combat action in the traditional sense, but a political-military operation, with certain restrictions being placed upon the military commanders, putting them at a tactical disadvantage. U.S forces had the clearly identifiable mission during the initial days of the crisis of protecting and evacuating U.S. and foreign nationals. This was to change later as political considerations created by U.S. and OAS policies clouded their mission. Military commanders, both on the scene and those in high positions in Washington, had to be prepared to exercise judgment in both military and political fields. It became apparent that military commanders, in addition to being competent in their own military fields, have to be prepared to take on the trappings of a diplomat

The third lesson to appear was the requirement for a more expanded intelligence effort. In addition to the customary military intelligence, there is a definite need for information on urban areas and the critical areas governing the control of an urban society   The important installations, together with biographical data on indigenous personages indicating their political tendencies and abilities, is required in the control of the civilian populace. It was quite

54

obvious that information media such as radio and television, as well as newspapers, can assist the psychological and propaganda effort of a military operation. This is particularly true in an area where a large portion of the involved population is illiterate. In conjunction with the information media, public services such as water supply, electric power, administrative and police apparatus, and banking facilities become important in providing for the welfare of the people.

Finally, the last lesson, but the most important to emerge, was the particular characteristic inherent in today's limited and cold war operations, a need for a reliable communication system In addition to the normal command and control channels, political considerations lead to detailed manipulation of the military forces from the highest levels of government. This requires a more sophisticated communications system within the objective area

It was indeed fortunate in the DomRep operation that CJTF-122 was on the scene and possessed adequate communications onboard the flagship to handle the situation. There was a period of seven days before USComDomRep was in any position to operate independently under the unified commander Had heavy fighting been encountered initially, adequate communications and ground control would have been more difficult to establish There is a definite need for a complete command and control system early in an operation. This requirement for a mobile command, control, and communication system can best be accomplished in an amphibious deployment by having the overall commander embarked in a ship with this capability. Alternative methods providing for a comparable communication link need to be devised for airlift expeditions.

The Ready Amphibious Squadron with the embarked 6th MEU proved the value of having a force prepared to effect a speedy response to any contingency situation. This is especially true in Latin America where coups and rumors are commonplace and where emergencies can occur with little or no warning This Ready Force was alerted on 25 April and within 17 hours was in position off Santo Domingo, standing by to assist in evacuation operations and to provide security to the U.S. Embassy. This demonstrated the importance of maintaining an immediate reaction force in the Caribbean area to cope with a variety of contingencies and also to provide the necessary initial communication and headquarters facilities.

From 25 April to 6 June, 7,958 combat-ready Marines were committed to the operation. During the entire period ashore the 4th MEB maintained the capability of re-embarking on board the amphibious shipping in the area to meet any new contingency that might arise.

General Bruce Palmer, USComDomRep, in commenting on the DomRep operation stated.

This was a joint team effort in DomRep and there ample glory for all services. I was particularly happy for the opportunity to command Marine Forces who lived up to my expectations. Our relationships with the initial joint task force and follow-on supporting naval task forces were extremely close and left nothing to be desired. From an Army point of view, the Air Force effort was fundamental because the very presence of Army forces was due to the initial air lift Here again, the team effort was cordial and close. . . .[71]

Notes

1. Unless otherwise noted, the material in this section is derived from: *ConTIC DomRep Study*; Committee on Foreign Affairs, *Latin American Documents*; Kurzman, *Santo Domingo Revolt*. Short titles of documents and published works cited are listed in Appendix A, Bibliography.

2 Committee on Foreign Affairs, *Latin American Documents*, p. 12

3. *Ibid.*, p. 28.

4 *Ibid* , p. 30.

5. *Ibid.*, p. 87

6. *Ibid* , p 213

7. *Ibid.*

8. *Ibid.*, p. 58.

9. The Inter-American Defense Board, whose purpose is to plan the collective defense of the Americas against outside aggression, was funded by the OAS, but never utilized as a military advisory staff. An Advisory Defense Committee, provided for at the OAS meeting at Bogota in 1948 "to advise the Organ of Consultation [Foreign Ministers of the OAS] on problems of military co-operation," was never organized. Stamey, *IADB*, pp. 41, 157. In effect, only the United States, by virtue of the presence of powerful military, naval, and air forces deployed to contain Cuban aggression, had such a ready force in the field in the 1960s.

10. Unless otherwise noted the material in this section is derived from: *JCS 2338/13-2; ConTIC DomRep Stud; FMFLant DomRep Study*; Kurzman, *Santo Domingo Revolt*; Black, "DomRep Crisis Management."

11. *ConTIC DomRep Study*, p. 8.

12. APCJ, the 14th of June movement, and extreme leftist Castroite group; MPD, Dominican Popular Movement, another Castroite party; and PSPD, Dominican Popular Socialist Party, the regular Communist party.

13. Kurzman, *Santo Domingo Revolt*, p. 129.

14. *Ibid.*, pp. 130-131.

15. *Ibid*, pp. 131-132.

16. *Ibid*, p. 137.

17. *Ibid.*, p. 133

18. Unless otherwise noted, the material in this section is derived from: *JCS 2338/13-3; JCS 2338/13-2; CinCLantFlt OpO 38-Yr, FMFLant OpO OP03100.4; 6th MEU ComdD, 6th MEU AfterExrRpt; BLT 3/6 ComdD; ProvMag-60 ComdD; MCCC Items*; Tompkins, "Ubique."

19. *FMFLant OP03100.4.*

20. *4th MEB AFtrExrRpt.*

21. *MCCC Items* and *BLT 3/6 ConD*, p. 2.

22. *6th MEU ComdD*, p. 2.

23. *6th MEU AfterExrRpt*

24. *4th MEB AFterExr Rpt.*

25. Unless otherwise noted, the material in this section is derived from: *JCS 2338/13-2; JCS 2338/13-3; MCCC Items; CJTF-122 Rpt; 4th MEB ComdD; 6th MEU ComdD; ProvMag-60 ComdD, 6th MEU ExrRpt, BLT 3/6 ComdD,* Tompkins, "Ubique"; Lann, *Crisis; DomRep ActRpt.*

26. JCS msg 251432Z April 1965 in *JCS 2338/13-2.*

27. JCS msg 262345Z April 1965 in *JCS 2338/13-3.*

28. The Hotel Embajador is the largest hotel in Santo Domingo, located approximately three miles from the heart of the city, near the seacoast Next to the hotel is a golf course and a polo field ideally suited as a helicopter landing zone.
   The Port of Haina is located 8 miles southwest of Santo Domingo at the mouth of the Rio Haina The port is connected to Santo Domingo by the four-lane Carretera Sanchez highway

29..JCS msg 271657Z April 1965 in *MCCC Items*

30. *6th MEU ComdD,* p 5

31. *Ibid.*

32. The Haina Landing Zone (LZ-6) was located in an open area, east of the Rio Haina, where the river changes its southerly course. It was generally rectangular with north-south legs 1,200 yards in length and east-west legs 500 yards in length. The only obstructions were patches of trees which could be bypassed.

33. *ProvMAG-60 ComdD*, p. 5.

34. *Ibid.*

35. AmEmb, SD 282040Z April 1965 msg in *JCS 2338/13-3*.

36. LZ-4 consisted of two polo fields just southwest of the Embajador Hotel, encompassing an area of about 400 square yards, all usable There were no landing obstructions to troop movement. Several highways to the northwest gave access to Avenida Angelita and to the city.

37 DefCon-2 is an increased readiness posture which is less than maximum readiness Designated military deployments and civil action may be necessary in line with the 'command's mission. Resources may be made available from outside the command. Forces are prepared for rapid transition to maximum readiness, if required Upon declaration of this DefCon an emergency conference by the JCS will be automatically convened to consider the establishment of H-hour for SIOP forces or other appropriate action.

38. *BLT 3/6 ComdD*, p. 5

39. VMFA-323 ComdD, p. 2.

40. Red Beach located 13.5 miles southwest of Santo Domingo at the mouth of the Rio Haina. There are two breakwaters at the river mouth with navigation lights at each end of the breakwaters. The length of the beach is 1,500 meters, all usable, width 95 meters. There is a gentle beach gradient 1:60, sand firm, trafficability good. Troops may exit at any point. Escarpment breached by three roads. All vehicle exits lead to a four-lane highway-Carretera Sanchez.

41. *BLT 3/6 ComdD*, p. 8

42. Unless otherwise noted, the material in this section is derived from: *JCS 2338/13-2, JCS 2338/13-3; MCCC Items, CJTF-122 Rpt; 4th MEB ComdD; 6th MEU ComdD; ProvMag-60 ComdD; 6th MEU ExrRpt; BLT 3/6 ComdD;* Tompkins, "Ubique"; and *DomRep Act Rpt.*

43. See Table of Organization, Appendix D.

44. *CJTF-122 Rpt*, pp. 1-3.

45. *CJTF-122 Rpt*, pp. I-6, 7 and II-2.

46. Objective "C" was located about a block and a half north of the U.S. Embassy at the intersection of Avenida Francia and Calle Leopoldo M. Navarro.
    Objective "D" was located about five blocks north of the U.S. Embassy at the intersection of Avenida La Esperilla and Dr. Guerrero.

47. Objective "B" was located approximately three blocks south of the U.S Embassy at the intersection of Avenida Bolivar and Calle Socorro Sanchez.

48. Objective "A" was located four blocks south of objective "B" at the intersection of Avenida Independencia and Calle Socorro Sanchez.

49. In DefCon 3, all designated forces would assume an increased posture above that of normal readiness, with the forces and resources for assuming increased posture normally coming within the command. All plans for the next higher condition of readiness were to be reviewed and made ready. No measures would be taken which would be considered provocative or which might compromise or disclose overall operational plans All commanders should time phase their actions in a manner to avoid speculation if possible.

50. DefCon 5. A normal readiness posture is directed toward maintaining optimum condition of combat readiness under routine training and operations. Unless a higher condition of readiness is directed, DefCon 5 shall be maintained in LantCom.

51 Unless otherwise noted, the material contained in this section is derived from· *JCS 2338/13-2; JCS 2338/13-3; CJT-122 Rpt*.

52. Unless otherwise noted, the material contained in this section is derived from *CJTF-122 Rpt; Dept of State Bulletins*.

53. "Secretary Rusk's News Conference of May 26, 1965," *The Department of State Bulletin*, June 14, 1965, p 941.

54. *CJTF-122 Rpt*, I-11.

55. Statement made by Amb Bunker, on 18 May, in plenary session of the Tenth Meeting of the Consultation of Ministers of Foreign Affairs of the American Republics.

56. Unless otherwise noted, the material in this section is derived from: *JCS 2338/13-3; BLT 3/6 ComdD; 4th MEB ComdD; BLT 1/2 ComdD; MCCC Items; BLT 1/8 ComD; CinCLant Resume, ProvMag-60 ComdD, VMFA-323 ComdD,* and *CO, MD, Newport News Rpt.*

57. JCS msg 042149Z May 1965, in *JCS 2338/13-3*.

58. CG, 2d MarDiv msg 080029Z May 1965 in *MCCC Items*.

59. *JCS 2338/13-3*, p. II-8

60. Unless otherwise noted, the material in this section is derived from: *JCS 2338/13-2; JCS 2338/13-3*; and *Dept of State Bulletin May-June 1965*.

61. Dept of State Bulletin, 31 May 1965, p 855.

62. *Ibid.*, p. 857.

63. The term Inter-American Force was changed to the InterAmerican Peace Force after the 22 May resolution was approved.

64. *Dept of State Bulletin*, 14 June 1965, p. 978

65. Unless otherwise noted, the material in this section is derived from: *4th MEB ComdD; ProvMag-60 ComdD; 6th MEU ComdD; BLT 3/6 ComdD, BLT 1/8 ComdD; BLT 1/6 ComdD; BLT 1/2 ComdD; 2/10 ComdD; MCCC Items*; and *VMFA(AW)-451 ComdD.*

66. *Dept of State Bulletin*, 31 May 1965, p. 862

67. CinCLant msg 082322Z May 1965

68. AmEmb, SD msg 230140Z May 1965 in *MCCC Items*.

69. These units consisted of: Det Hdqrs, 6th Mar; Hdqrs Btry, 2/10,. Det, MASS-1, Det, Co C, 2d MedBn; Hdqrs, Co B,2dTkBn; Hdqrs, Co B, 2d AT Bn; and Co A, 2d MedBn

70. Unless otherwise noted, the material in this section is derived from· *JCS 2338/13-3; 4th MEB ComdD; 4th MEB AR; CinCLant Resume*; and *ProvMAG-60 ComdD.*

71. *Palmer Rpt*, Vol I, Tab C.

Appendix A

Bibliography

Note: Only paragraphs, messages, and entries classified SECRET and below have been used from sources classified TOP SECRET overall

Documents:

Joint Chiefs of Staff 2338/13-2, Lessons Learned in the Dominican Republic Operations, dtd 26 May 1965, hereafter *JCS 2338/13-2*.

Joint Chiefs of Staff 2338/13-3, Lessons Learned in the Dominican Republic (Final Report), dtd 30 Nov 1965, hereafter *JCS 2338/13-3*

Marine Corps Command Center, Items of Significant Interest April-June 1965, hereafter *MCCC Items*

Headquarters, U S. Marine Corps, Readiness Staff Journal, 012200R May-061400R May, hereafter *HQMC Jnl*

Commander-in-Chief, Atlantic, Operation Plan 310/2-64, Dominican Republic, downgraded by CinCLant 012300Z May 1965, hereafter *CinCLant OPlan 310/2-64*

Commander-in-Chief, Atlantic msg to Joint Chiefs of Staff, dtd 261438Z June 1965, Subj: Resume and Analysis of Dominican Republic Operation, hereafter *CinCLant Resume.*

Fleet Marine Force, Atlantic, Amphibious Area Study-3, Dominican Republic, dtd 15 June 1961, hereafter *FMFLant DomRep Study*.

Tactical Intelligence Center, U.S. Continental Army Command, ConTIC Country Study-Dominican Republic, dtd April 1965, hereafter *ConTIC DomRep Study* (NOFORN)

Commander, Joint Task Force, 122/Commander Second Fleet, Report of Operation Power Pack, 28 April-May 1965, dtd 9 May 1965, hereafter *CJTF-122 Rpt.*

LtGen Bruce Palmer, Jr., USA, Report of Stability Operations, Dominican Republic, dtd 31 August 1965, hereafter *Palmer Rpt*

4th Marine Expeditionary Brigade, Command Diary, 29 April-6 June 1965, dtd 21 June 1965, hereafter *4th MEB ComdD*.

4th Marine Expeditionary Brigade, Action Report, 29 April-6 June 1965, dtd 25 June 1965, hereafter *4th MEB AR*.

4th Marine Expeditionary Brigade, Training Exercise Report, dtd 26 April 1965, hereafter *4th MEB ExrRpt*.

6th Marine Expeditionary Unit, Final Exercise Report, dtd 19 June 1965, hereafter *6th MEU ExrRpt*.

6th Marine Expeditionary Unit, Command Diary, 2 April-1 July 1965, dtd 9 July 1965, hereafter *6th MEU ComdD*.

Provisional Marine Aircraft Group 60, Command Diary, 8 December 1964-28 June 1965, hereafter *ProvMag-60 ComdD*

1st Battalion, 2d Marines, Command Diary, 30 April-2 June 1965, hereafter *BLT 1/2 ComdD*

1st Battalion, 6th Marines, Command Diary, dtd 30 June 1965, hereafter *BLT 1/6 ComdD*.

3d Battalion, 6th Marines, Command Diary, 1 February-1 July 1965, dtd 9 August 1965, hereafter *BLT 3/6 ComdD*.

1st Battalion, 8th Marines, Command Diary, 2 May-2 June 1965, dtd 17 June 1965, hereafter *BLT 1/8 ComdD*

2d Battalion, 10th Marines, Command Diary, 28 April-6 June 1965, dtd 21 June 1965, hereafter *2/10 ComdD*.

Marine Medium Helicopter Squadron 263, Command Diary, 30 April-29 May 1965, dtd 30 June 1965, hereafter *HMM-263 ComdD*.

Marine Medium Helicopter Squadron 264, Command Diary, 2 April-28 June 1965, dtd 8 July 1965, hereafter *HMM-264 ComdD*.

Marine Fighter/Attack Squadron 323, Command Diary, 13 March-10 May 1965, dtd 4 June 1965, hereafter *VMFA-323 ComdD*

Marine All-Weather Fighter Squadron 451, Command Diary, 28 April-31 May 1965, dtd 22 June 1965, hereafter *VMF(AW)-451 ComdD*

FMFLant OP03100.4, *Standard Operating Procedure for Caribbean Deployment*, 25 Nov 1964.

Marine Detachment, USS *Newport News* (CA-148), Command Chronology, 1 July-31 December 1965, dtd 8 March 1966, hereafter *MD Newport News Rpt*.

Published Works:

Black, John T., "Problems of Crisis Management: Dominican Republic." *Armed Forces Management*, Vol. II, No. 10 (Jul 65), hereafter Black, "DomRep Crisis Management."

Berger, Paul A , GySgt, USMC, "The Corridor," *Leatherneck*, Vol. XLIX, No. 8 (Aug 65), hereafter Berger, "The Corridor."

.... "Peace Force: On Line," *Leatherneck*, Vol XLIX, No. 8 (Aug 65), hereafter Berger, "Peace Force."

Dare, James A., Captain, USN, "Dominican Diary", *U.S. Naval Institute Proceedings*, Vol. 91, No. 12 (Dec 65), hereafter Dare, "Dominican Diary."

Kurzman, Dan. *Santo Domingo: Revolt of the Damned* (New York· G. P. Putnam's Sons, 1965), hereafter Kurzman, *Santo Domingo Revolt*.

Lann, Fred. "Crisis in the Caribbean-I," *QST*, Vol. XLIV, No. 9 (Sept 65), hereafter Lann, "Crisis."

Stamey, Roderick A., LtCol, USA, *The Inter-American Defense Board* (Washington: Office of the Chief of Military History, Department of the Army, 1965), hereafter Stamey, IADB.

Szulc, Ted. *Dominican Diary* (New York Delacorte Press 1965), hereafter Szulc, *Dominican Diary*.

Tompkins, Rathvon, McC , MajGen, USMC. "Ubique," *Marine Corps Gazette*, Vol. 49, No. 9 (Sept 65), hereafter Tompkins, "Ubique."

Committee on Foreign Affairs, House of Representatives, 89th Congress, 2d Session, *Regional and Other Documents Concerning United States Relations with Latin America*. (Washington. Government Printing Office, 1966), hereafter Committee on Foreign Affairs, *Latin American Documents*.

U.S. Department of State, *U.S. Department of State Bulletin*, April-June 1965, Washington: Government Printing Office, 1965, hereafter *Dept of State Bulletin*.

The Center for Strategic Studies, Georgetown University, *Dominican Action--
1965*, Washington, D.C., July 1966, hereafter CSS, *Dominican Action.*

Appendix B

COMMAND AND STAFF LIST
4TH MARINE EXPEDITIONARY BRIGADE
AS OF 14 MAY 1965

Commanding General . . . . Gen John G. Bouker
Chief of Staff . . . . Col Kenneth L. Reusser
G-1 . . . . LtCol John J. Swords
G-2 . . . . LtCol Bertram H. Curwen, Jr
G-3 . . . . LtCol David E Lownds
G-4 . . . . LtCol Harvey E. Spielman

6th MEU (6th Marines)

Commanding Officer . . . . Col George W Daughtry
Executive Officer . . . . LtCol Harold N. Mehaffey
S-3 . . . . Maj Stephen G Olmstead

Battalion Landing Team 1/6

Commanding Officer . . . . LtCol William F. Doehler
Executive Officer . . . . Maj George T Sargent
S-3 . . . . Maj Karl E. Moore

Commanding Officer
Headquarters and Service
Company . . . . Capt John G. Flynn

Commanding Officer
Company A . . . . Capt Merle G. Sorenson

Commanding Officer
Company B . . . . Capt Richard L. Evans

Commanding Officer
Company C . . . . Capt Donald F. Tremmel

Commanding Officer
Company D . . . . Capt John J. Rozman

Commanding Officer . . . . LtCol Poul F. Pedersen
Executive Officer . . . . Maj Joseph J. Gambardella
S-3 . . . . Maj Henry V. Martin

Commanding Officer
Headquarters and Service
Company . . . . Capt Donald Festa

Commanding Officer
Company I . . . . Capt William G. Davis

Commanding Officer
Company K . . . . Capt Robert C. Cockell

Commanding Officer
Company L . . . . Capt Horace W Baker

Commanding Officer
Company M (Gitmo) . . . . Capt Paul A Wilson Jr.

Battalion Landing Team 1/8

Commanding Officer . . . . LtCol Edward F. Danowitz
Executive Officer . . . . Maj Robert E Hill
S-3 . . . . Maj Marvin H. Lugger

Commanding Officer
Headquarters and Service
Company . . . . Capt Russell I Hudson

Commanding Officer
Company A . . . . Capt Joseph Loughran

Commanding Officer
Company B . . . . 1stLt Donald B Evans

Commanding Officer
Company C . . . . Capt Paul K Dougherty

Commanding Officer
Company D . . . . Capt Charles Barstow

Battalion Landing Team 1/2 (Reserve)

Commanding Officer . . . . LtCol James E. Harrell
Executive Officer . . . . Maj Earl F. Roth
S-3 . . . . Maj John A. Sparks

Commanding Officer
Headquarters and Service
Company . . . . 1stLt William J. Hayes III

Commanding Officer
Company A . . . . Capt Robert C. Knowles

Commanding Officer
Company B . . . . Capt Arthur P. Brill Jr.

Commanding Officer
Company C . . . . Capt Edmund Keefe Jr.

Commanding Officer
Company D . . . . 1stLt Robert J O'Brien

2d Battalion, 10th Marines

2d Battalion, 10th Marines
Commanding Officer . . . . Maj Kenneth C. Williams
Executive Officer . . . . Maj Alva F. Thompson
S-3 . . . . Maj George T. Hoagland

Commanding Officer
Headquarters Btry . . . . 1stLt Joseph M. Warren

Commanding Officer
Howtar Btry, 2/10 . . . . 1stLt George V. Thurmond
          (1-20 May)
. . . . 1stLt Herbert W. Degraff
          (20-29 May)

Commanding Officer
Howtar Btry, 3/10 . . . . 1stLt Sidney B. Grimes
          (29 April-26 May)
. . . . 1stLt Thomas E. Mossy
          (27 May-6 June)

Commanding Officer
Btry E . . . . Capt Joseph C. Mayers

Commanding Officer
Btry F . . . . Capt William D. Benjamin

Prov MAG-60

Commanding Officer . . . . LtCol James E. Fegley
OpnsO . . . . Maj Robert A. Plamondon

VMF(AW)-451

Commanding Officer . . . . LtCol Dellwyn L. Davis

VMFA-323

Commanding Officer . . . . LtCol Norman W. Gourley

HMM-263

Commanding Officer . . . . LtCol Truman Clark

HMM-264

Commanding Officer . . . . LtCol Frederick M. Kleppsattel Jr.

Logistical Support Group

Commanding Officer . . . . Maj Joseph F. Schoen Jr.

Appendix C

List of Marine Units Eligible for the Armed Forces Expeditionary Medal, Dominican Republic (28 April-10 June 1965)

4th Marine Expeditionary Brigade

Headquarters, 4th Marine Expeditionary Brigade

  Sub Unit 1, Headquarters Company, Headquarters Battalion, 4th MEB
  Detachment, Headquarters Battalion, 2d Marine Division
  Detachment, 2d Marine Aircraft Wing
  Detachment, Headquarters Battery, 10th Marines
  Detachment, 42d Civil Affairs Company (US Army)
  Detachment, Headquarters Company, 8th Communications Battalion
  Detachment, 2d Radio Battalion
  Detachment, Engineer Company, 2d Engineer Battalion
  Detachment, 2d Reconnaissance Battalion
  Sub Unit 1, Headquarters and Headquarters Squadron 27
  Detachment, Headquarters and Service Company, 2d Service Battalion
  Detachment, Marine Wing Headquarters Group 2
  Detachment, Marine Fighter Squadron 235
  Detachment, Headquarters and Maintenance Squadron 14, Marine Aircraft
    Group 14
  Detachment, Headquarters and Service Company, Supply Battalion, 2d
    Force Service Regiment
  Detachment, 8th Motor Transport Battalion
  Detachment, Headquarters Company, Force Troops
  Detachment, Support Company, Headquarters and Service Battalion, 2d
    Force Service Regiment
  Detachment, Headquarters, Force Troops
  Detachment, Headquarters and Headquarters Squadron 2, Marine Wing
    Headquarters Group 2
  Detachment, 8th Engineer Battalion
  Communications Support Company, 8th Communications Battalion

Brigade Engineer Group

  Company B (-), 2d Engineer Battalion
  1st Platoon, Company C, 2d Engineer Battalion
  3d Platoon, Company C, 2d Engineer Battalion

Detachment, 1st Platoon, Company A, 2d Engineer Battalion
Detachment, Engineer Support Company, 2d Engineer Battalion
1st Platoon (Rein), Company C, 8th Engineer Battalion

Company C (Rein), 2d Medical Battalion

Company C, 2d Medical Battalion
Surgical Team
Detachment, Water Supply Section, 2d Engineer Battalion

Headquarters Company (-) (Rein), 6th Marines

Sub Unit 1, Headquarters Company, 6th Marines
Detachment, Headquarters, Force Troops
Detachment, Headquarters, FMFLant
Detachment, Communications Company, Headquarters Battalion
Detachment, 2d Battalion, 10th Marines

1st Battalion (-), 6th Marines

Headquarters and Service Company
Company A
Company B
Company C
Company D
Detachment, Marine Heavy Helicopter Squadron 461, Marine Aircraft
    Group 26
Detachment, Headquarters Company, Headquarters Battalion
Detachment, Service Company, Headquarters Battalion

3d Battalion (-), 6th Marines

Headquarters and Service Company
Company I
Company K
Company L
Detachment, Battery E, 2d Battalion, 10th Marines
Detachment, Headquarters Battery, 2d Battalion, 10th Marines
Detachment, Headquarters Battery, 10th Marines
2d Platoon, Company B, 2d Reconnaissance Battalion
Detachment, 2d Force Service Regiment
Detachment, Headquarters and Service Battalion, Marine Corps Base

1st Battalion (-), 8th Marines

    Headquarters and Service Company
    Company A
    Company B
    Company C
    Company D
    Detachment, Headquarters Battalion
    Detachment, 2d Reconnaissance Battalion
    Detachment, 2d Engineer Battalion
    Detachment, 1st Battalion, 10th Marines
    Detachment, Howtar Battery, 3d Battalion, 10th Marines

Logistical Support Group

    Detachment, Company A, 2d Shore Party Battalion
    Detachment, Headquarters and Service Company, 2d Shore Party Battalion
    Detachment, Company B, 2d Shore Party Battalion
    Company C (-) (Rein), 2d Shore Party Battalion
      Detachment, Headquarters and Service Company, 2d Shore Party Battalion
    Detachment, 2d Service Battalion
      Detachment, Headquarters and Service Company
      Detachment, Truck Company
      Detachment, Maintenance Company
      Detachment, Supply Company
    Company B (-), 2d Motor Transport Battalion
    1st Platoon, Company D, 8th Motor Transport Battalion
    Detachment, 2d Force Service Regiment
      Detachment, Bulk Fuel Company
      Detachment, Motor Transport Maintenance Company, Maintenance
        Battalion
      Detachment, Ordnance Company, Maintenance Battalion
      Detachment, Communications Company, Headquarters and Service
        Battalion
      Detachment, Electronics Maintenance Company
      Detachment, Supply Company, Supply Battalion
      Detachment, Truck Company, Headquarters and Service Battalion
      Detachment, Headquarters Company, Supply Battalion
      Headquarters Company, Headquarters and Service Battalion
      Detachment, Support Company, Headquarters and Service Battalion
    Detachment, Naval Beach Group 2
      Detachment, Headquarters Group
      Detachment, Beach Party Team 2
      Detachment, Beach Party Team 3
      Detachment, Causeway Detachment

Company I (-), 3d Battalion, 6th Marines

4th Marine Expeditionary Brigade Reserve

1st Battalion (-) (Rein), 2d Marines

  Headquarters and Service Company
  Company A
  Company B
  Company C
  Company D
  2d Platoon, Company C, 2d Reconnaissance Battalion
  Detachment, Headquarters Battalion
  Howtar Battery, 2d Battalion, 10th Marines
  Detachment, Headquarters Company, 2d Marines
  Detachment, Headquarters Company, 2d Battalion, 10th Marines
  Detachment, Company A, 2d Engineer Battalion
  Detachment, Company C, 2d Anti-Tank Battalion
  Detachment, Company A, 2d Motor Transport Battalion
  Detachment, 2d Service Battalion
  Detachment, Company A, 2d Amphibian Tractor Battalion
  Detachment, Truck Company, 2d Force Service Regiment
  Detachment, Bulk Fuel Company, 2d Force Service Regiment
  Detachment, Support Company, 2d Force Service Regiment
  Detachment, Ordnance Maintenance Company, 2d Force Service Regiment
  Detachment, 2d Motor Transport Battalion
  Detachment, 2d Force Service Regiment
  Detachment, 2d Service Battalion, Force Service Regiment
  Detachment, Headquarters Battalion
  Company A, 2d Medical Battalion
  Company C, (-), (Rein), 8th Engineer Battalion
  Company A, (-), 2d Amphibian Tractor Battalion
  Detachment, 2d Amphibian Tractor Battalion
  Detachment, 2d Tank Battalion
  Detachment, 2d Anti-Tank Battalion

2d Battalion (-) (Rein), 10th Marines

  Headquarters Battery
  Battery E
  Battery F
  Howtar Battery, 3d Battalion, 10th Marines

Company C (-) (Rein), 2d Reconnaissance Battalion

Company B (-) (Rein), 2d Anti-Tank Battalion

Company B (-) (Rein), 2d Tank Battalion

1st Platoon (Rein), Company A, 2d Amphibian Tractor Battalion

Detachment, Headquarters Battery, 10th Marines (NAO)

Provisional Marine Aircraft Group 60

Headquarters, Provisional Marine Aircraft Group 60
Operations Section
Air Control Section
Detachment, Marine Air Support Squadron 1
Detachment, Air Delivery Platoon, 2d Force Service Regiment
Detachment, Marine Air Base Squadron 27, Marine Wing Service Group 1
(Air Freight)
Communications Section

Marine Medium Helicopter Squadron 263 (Rein)
Detachment, Marine Heavy Helicopter Squadron 461
Detachment, Marine Observation Squadron 1
Detachment, Marine Air Base Squadron 26
Detachment, Headquarters and Maintenance Squadron 26
Sub Unit 1, Service Maintenance Squadron
Detachment, 2d Force Reconnaissance Company

Marine Medium Helicopter Squadron 264 (Rein)
Detachment, Marine Observation Squadron 1
Detachment, Heavy Helicopter Squadron 461
Detachment, Marine Composite Reconnaissance Squadron 2
Detachment, Marine Air Base Squadron 26
Detachment, 2d Force Reconnaissance Company
Detachment, Service Maintenance Squadron, Cherry Point
Sub Unit 1, Headquarters and Headquarters Squadron 27
Headquarters and Maintenance Squadron 26

Marine All-Weather Fighter Squadron 451 (Roosevelt Roads)
Marine Fighter Squadron 323
Marine Aerial Refueler Transport Squadron 252

Appendix D

CHRONOLOGY

U.S. Marine Corps Operations in the Dominican Republic
April-June 1965

Selected events bearing on the Marine Corps involvement in the Dominican Republic have been included for the periods before and after the actual service of Marine Corps units ashore at Santo Domingo. Sources for the chronological entries include both messages and reports, as well as several published first-hand accounts of operations. Where messages are taken from reports, the location is shown. Short titles have been used to identify sources; the bibliography of this study includes the full titles. Where time is shown, the time zone is R, the zone that includes the Dominican Republic and the east coast of the United States. In all cases, the time of the messages and reports has been converted to R time.

Date	Item
26Jan65	At 1335R, FMFLant authorized the activation of CARIB 2-65 for planning and established the major elements, effective 1Feb65. *AdminLant 261835Z in BLT 3/6 ComdD*
28Jan65	At 1449R, CG 2d MarDiv authorized activation of the 6th MEU, effective 1Feb65, for planning and subsequent deployment as an element of CARIB 2-65. *CG 2d MarDiv 281949Z in 6th MEU AfterExrRpt*
1Feb65	CO 6th MEU reported to ComPhibRon 10 for planning and subsequent deployment as an element of CARIB 2-65, CO Prov-MAG-60 reported to CO 6th MEU for planning and subsequent operations as an element of 6th MEU. *CG 2d MarDiv 012216Z in 6th MEU AfterExrRpt*
3Feb65	CO BLT 3/6 reported to CO 6th MEU for planning and subsequent operations as an element of 6th MEU. *CO BLT 3/6 031845Z in 6th MEU AfterExrRpt*

9Feb65	.Exercise QUICK KICK VII preliminary conference held at Head-quarters, ComPhibRon 4 (CG 4th MEB and CO 6th MEU attended). *ComPhibRon 4 051631Z in 6th MEU AfterExrRpt*
24Feb65	CO ProvMAG-60 reported to ,CG 4th MEB for planning and operations in QUICK KICK VII *ProvMAG-60 ComdD*
26Feb65	CO 3d Bn, 6th Mar reported to CO RLT-6 (CO 6th MEU) for planning and operations in QUICK KICK VII. *CO 3/6 261810Z in 6th MEU AfterExrRpt*
1Mar65	CO BLT 3/8 reported to CO RLT-6 for planning and operations in QUICK KICK VII. *CO BLT 3/8 011806Z in 6th MEU AfterExrRpt*
3Mar65	CO LSU. 6th MEU provided by 2d SP Bn *6th MEU AfterExrRpt*
22Mar65	CO RLT-6 reported to opcon CG 4th MEB for QUICK KICK VII. *CO RLT-6 222256Z in 6th MEU AfterExrRpt*
30Mar65	6th MEU began embarkation at Morehead City for CARIB 2-65 (including QUICK KICK VII). *6th MEU AfterExrRpt*
2Apr65	6th MEU completed loading PhibRon 10 shipping at Morehead City and Onslow Beach. *6th MEU AfterExrRpt* Hq 4th MEB, Hq ProvMAG-60, and Hq LSG 4th embarked AGC *Taconic* at Morehead City for QUICK KICK VII *CG 4th MEB 011824Z in MCCC Items*
3Apr65	At 0001R, CARIB 2-65 Ready Group, 6th MEU in shipping of PhibRon 10, departed Morehead City. *CTG 181.1 030320Z in MCCC Items*
7Apr65	Turnaway rehearsal off Vieques for QUICK KICK VII using helicopters of HMM-262 (LPH *Guadalcanal*) and HMM-264 (LPH *Boxer*). *ProvMAG-60 ComdD*
9Apr65	At 0630R, QUICK KICK VII began with 4th MEB landing by sea and air on Vieques; 3d Brig, 82d AbnDiv air dropped as part of the exercise. *MCCC Items; BLT 3/6 ComdD*
10Apr65	At 1715R, QUICK KICK VII secured by CG 4th MEB after link-up of BLT 3/6 and 3d Brig, 82d AbnDiv. *6th MEU ComdD*

11Apr65	Reembarkation of 4th MEB elements completed; 6th MEU reconstituted at 1300R, 4th MEB units and headquarters augmentation sailed for ConUS. *ProvMAG-60 ComdD; 6th MEU ComdD*
12Apr65	CARIB 2-65 arrived at Guantanamo Bay; M/3/6 landed as defense augmentation ready force. *BLT 3/6 ComdD*
13-16 Apr65	6th MEU liberty at Guantanamo Bay; concurrent orientation of key personnel on base defenses. *6th MEU ComdD*
17Apr65	CARIB 2-65 Ready Group (TG 44.9) departed Guantanamo Bay for Exercise PLACE KICK. *BLT 3/6 ComdD*
19Apr65	At 0730R, PLACE KICK began with 6th MEU landing by sea and air on Vieques; exercise secured at 0945R and 6th MEU moved to Camp Garcia, reporting to opcon CG 2d MarDiv. *6th MEU ComdD*
20-23 Apr65	6th MEU conducted small unit training and familiarization firing of weapons at Camp Garcia, on 23 April BLT 3/6 conducted a firing exercise with close air support by VMFA-323. *BLT 3/6 ComdD*
23Apr65	At 0800R, 1st Bn, 6th Mar assumed duties as 2d MarDiv Airlift Alert Bn; Alpha Increment (C/1/6) assumed Alert Condition II, capable of leaving Camp Lejeune for Cherry Point within 5 1/2 hours. *1/6 ComdD*
24Apr65	At 0700R, 6th MEU began reembarkation on ships of PhibRon 10; reembarkation completed by 1600R and CO 6th MEU reported to opcon CTG 44.9. *6th MEU ComdD*
	At 1914R, CinCLantFlt began getting reports of riots, demonstrations, and an attempted coup in Santo Domingo from AmEmb Santo Domingo; at 2226R, these reports were passed to CTG 44.9 with advice that no action was required at this time. *Tompkins, Ubique*
25Apr65	At 1007R, as a result of the deteriorating situation in DomRep, CinCLantFlt directed CTG 44.9 to move toward DomRep; ships were underway prior to 1100R. *CinCLantFlt 251407Z in MCCC Items; Dare, Dominican Diary*
	At 1032R, the JCS directed CinCLant to position TG 44.9 off the southwest coast of DomRep, out of sight of land, prepared to evacuate U.S Nationals. *JCS 251432Z in MCCC Items*

En route to DomRep, CO 6th MEU issued a warning order for possible evacuation operations and formulated an operation plan in conjunction with CTG 44.9. *Dare, Dominican Diary; BLT 3/6 ComdD*

26Apr65   Between 0200R and 0700R, ships of TG 44.9, with an evacuation capacity of 3,600 persons, arrived on station off DomRep. *Dare, Dominican Diary, CinCLant 260002Z in MCCC Items*

At 1015R, 6th MEU assumed a two-hour alert status for evacuation operations. *6th MEU ComdD*

26Apr65   At 1030R, AmEmb Santo Domingo began advising U.S. citizens to prepare for evacuation with the Hotel Embajador the designated assembly point *AmEmb SD 261606Z in MCCC Items*

At 1849R, the JCS increased the readiness condition of the 3d Brig (2 BCTs), 82d AbnDiv, airlift as required, and command and support elements for possible employment in DomRep. *JCS 262349Z in JCS 2338/13-3*

About 2030R, AmEmb Santo Domingo requested evacuation of U.S. citizens from DomRep to begin 270600R; both sides in the fighting had agreed to a cease fire during evacuation operations *FoneCon NMCC 262146Q in MCCC Items*

27Apr65   At 0430R, 6th MEU assumed 15-minute alert status for evacuation operations. *6th MEU ComdD*

At 0600R, evacuees began assembling at the Hotel Embajador for processing by AmEmb personnel *Tompkins, Ubique*

At 1030R, two UH1Es, with CO, 6th MEU and CO, HMM-26 on board, were launched from LPH Boxer to escort the U.S. Ambassador from Punta Concedo International Airport to the *Boxer* and then to the port of Jaina. *6th MEU ComdD; ProvMAG-60 ComdD*

During the morning, ships of TG 44.9 closed to within five miles of the coast of DomRep; reports from AmEmb indicated evacuees at the Embajador Hotel were being threatened by rebel forces and that Jaina was the only safe evacuation point. *Dare, Dominican Diary*

At 1130R, 6th MEU Command Group reconnoitered the Jaina port area and helo landing zone. *6th MEU ComdD*

At 1157R, the JCS directed CinCLant to order CTG 44.9 to close DomRep and begin evacuating approximately 1,000 U.S. nationals; San Juan, P.R. was designated as safe haven for evacuees. *JCS 271657Z in MCCC Items*

At 1230R, Beach Control Unit, 6th MEU LSU established at Jaina to coordinate evacuee loading on the LST *Wood County* and APD *Ruchamkin*. *6th MEU ComdD*

At 1310R, the pathfinder element of HMM-264 and air control element of ProvMAG-60 landed at Jaina to establish a helo landing zone for evacuation operations. *6th MEU ComdD*

At 1400R, two unarmed squads of K/3/6 landed at Jaina to assist in the control of evacuees; at the same time the first evacuees arrived on the *Boxer*. *6th MEU ComdD*

At 1530, the first evacuees were loaded on board ship. *CinCLant Resume*

At 1655, a medical administrative team from BLT 3/6 was lifted to Jaina to provide medical assistance to evacuees. *6th MEU ComdD*

27Apr65 At 1700R, the *Ruchamkin* sailed with 200 evacuees and BLT 3/6 medical team, followed at 1740R by the *Wood County* with 420 evacuees. *BLT 3/6 ComdD; Dare, Dominican Diary*

By 1720R, helo evacuation from Jaina was completed and all Marines were back on board ship; 294 evacuees had been lifted to the *Boxer* and 264 to the LPD *Raleigh*. *ProvMAG-60 ComdD; Dare, Dominican Diary*

At 1830R, 6th MEU Command Group conducted a reconnaissance of the Jaina area for possible evacuee stragglers, none observed. *6th MEU ComdD*

During the day, CinCLant set DefCon 3 for selected naval forces for DomRep operations and designated ComSecondFlt as CJTF 122, CinCLant requested that CinCStrike designate forces (BCTs and TacAir) for DomRep operations and report their attainment of DefCon 3. *CinCLant Resume*

28Apr65   About 0900R, helo transfer of evacuees on *Boxer* to *Raleigh* began: transfer completed shortly before noon and *Raleigh* sailed for San Juan. *Dare, Dominican Diary*

At 1315R, the Ambassador relayed to Washington the request of the military junta that the United States lend "its immediate and unlimited military assistance" to prevent a Communist-dominated rebel takeover in DomRep. *AmEmb SD 282015Z in CJTF 122 Rpt*

At 1316R, an unarmed seven-man working party from BLT 3/6 was lifted to Jaina to assist in handling rations destined for AmEmb; the party returned at 1450R. *BLT 3/6 ComdD*

At 1330R, a medical/administrative team of BLT 3/6 was sent to Jaina to help organize and assist continued evacuation of civilians. *BLT 3/6 ComdD*

At 1540R, the Ambassador asked Washington to land Marines to insure the safety of evacuees and to reinforce the AmEmb guard in view of the continued sniping and disorder in the city. *AmEmb SD 282040Z in JCS 2338/13-3*

At 1615R, BLT 3/6 was alerted for a possible move ashore; *Boxer* units were issued a basic allowance of ammunition. *BLT 3/6 ComdD*

At 1700R, CG 2d MarDiv issued orders to 1/6 to move its Alpha airlift increment (C/1/6) to Cherry point; increment reached Cherry point at 1945R. *1/6 ComdD*

Continual liaison with the Ambassador by CO 6th MEU and CTG 44.9 indicated a steadily deteriorating situation ashore as the afternoon wore on; at 1740R, the Ambassador requested that a large group of evacuees be lifted from the Polo Grounds (LZ 4) near the Embajador and that an armed platoon be provided to reinforce the embassy guard. *6th MEU ComdD*

At 1740R, pathfinder elements and an unarmed platoon from K/3/6 were lifted to LZ 4 to assist in the evacuation of civilians. *HMM-264 ComdD; BLT 3/6 ComdD*

At 1747R, VMFA-323 at Roos Roads was ordered by ComCarib-SeaFron to prepare four aircraft with air to air and air to ground ordnance for missions over DomRep; alert status was later changed to unarmed strip alert for the night with armed strip alert for eight aircraft by 290345R. *VMFA-323 ComdD*

At 1815R, the Ambassador asked Washington to land all of the 6th MEU and move the two alerted airborne BCTs to DomRep to protect American lives *AmEmb SD 282315Z in JCS 2338/13-3*

At 1820R, an armed and reinforced platoon of L/3/6 was lifted to LZ 4, while these troops were airborne CTG 44.9 was authorized to land more Marines if the Ambassador requested them. *Dare, Dominican Diary; BLT 3/6 ComdD*

At 1830R, the remainder of L/3/6, less the ship's platoon, was lifted to LZ 4 to secure it for the landing of the rest of the BLT. *BLT 3/6 ComdD*

At 1915R, BLT 3/6 Command Group was airborne; it arrived at LZ 4 at 1940R. *BLT 3/6 ComdD*

At 2228R, CG FMFLant alerted CG 2d MarDiv to activate Headquarters, 4th MEB. *CG FMFLant 290328Z in G-3 Jnl, 4th MEB ComdD*

By 2330R, all *Boxer* units (536 Marines) were ashore; 684 evacuees had been lifted out on return flights. *BLT 3/6 ComdD; ProvMAG-60 ComdD*

By 2350R, all helos of HMM-264 were back on board *Boxer, Raleigh,* recalled when landing appeared imminent, arrived off Santo Domingo before evacuation/landing operation ended. *Dare, Dominican Diary; ProvMAG-60 ComdD*

29Apr65   At 0037R, a "clutch" platoon from H&S/3/6 was dispatched, at the Ambassador's request, to reinforce the AmEmb guard which was being harassed by snipers. *BLT 3/6 ComdD*

At 0445R, VMFA-323 launched one F4B for air control and weather reconnaissance over DomRep; armed CAP over ships off DomRep was flown beginning at 0759R *VMFA-323 ComdD*

At 0500R, VMF(AW)-451 at Roos Roads (relief for VMFA-323) assumed a one hour alert status; this was confirmed by ComCaribSeaFron at 0930R; squadron began flying CAP over ships off DomRep at 1230. *VMF(AW)-451 ComdD*

At 0545R, helo operations began for the day when two UH-34s lifted medical supplies from the Boxer to LZ 4 for issuance to Red

Cross and civilian medical agencies; helo supply operations, both civil relief and military, inbound and evacuee airlift outbound continued throughout the day. *ProvMAG-60 ComdD; BLT 3/6 ComdD*

At 0645R, 6th MEU Command Group landed in the AmEmb grounds for extensive conference with Embassy officials. *6th MEU ComdD*

At 0800R, CG 2d MarDiv directed the activation of Headquarters, 4th MEB for operations. *CG 2d MarDiv 290554Z in G-3 Jnl, 4th MEB ComdD*

At 0835R, Alpha increment of 1/6 was ordered airborne by CG 2d MarDiv, destination Guantanamo Bay; first plane lifted at 0940R, last at 1000R, with arrival at Guantanamo about 1430R. *CG 2d MarDiv 291530Z in G-4 Jnl, 4th MEB ComdD.*

At 1111R, ComCaribSeaFron directed DD *Roan* and DLG *Luce* to embark Alpha increment of 1/6, on its arrival at Guantanamo; CinCLant further directed that this unit be landed in DomRep as soon as possible, ETA 300300R. *ComCaribSeaFron 291611Z in CJTF 122 Rpt*

At 1343R, CG FMFLant directed CG 2d MAW to chop two RF8A to VMF(AW)-451 for photo reconnaissance, as requested by ComCaribSeaFront. *CG FMFLant 281843Z in MCCC Items*

At 1430R, CTG 44.9 and CO 6th MEU met with the Ambassador at the AmEmb to evaluate the worsening situation; Contact was made with Washington and "all present agreed to land the remainder of the Marines with heavy equipment over the beach." *Dare, Dominican Diary*

At 1423R, ComSecondFlt, after a plane flight to Puerto Rico and transfer to the DD *Leahy* arrived off DomRep, boarded the *Boxer*, and assumed command of all U.S. forces in the area as CJTF 122; he confirmed the decision to land the rest of 6th MEU, which had also been ordered by the JCS at 1511R *JCS 292011Z in MCCC Items; Tompkins, Ubique*

At 1502R, CinCLant, in response to a JCS directive, ordered two airborne BCTs at Pope AFB, North Carolina, to proceed to Ramey AFB, Puerto Rico, as soon as possible; the order provided for an assault air drop near San Isidro airbase in DomRep early on 30 April. *CinCLant 292002Z in CJTF 122 Rpt; Tompkins, Ubique*

At 1731R, remainder of BLT 3/6 began landing over Jaina beach, an infantry (I/3/6) and armor column immediately moved out to join the rest of the BLT at the Hotel Embajador - LZ 4 perimeter, arriving about 1830R. *BLT 3/6 ComdD*

At 1746, CG FMFLant outlined the major forces to be included in the 4th MEB to CinCLant as: Hq 4th MEB; Hq 6th Mar; BLT 1/6; BLT 3/6; BLT 2/2; ProvMAG-60 including HMM-264, HMM-263, VMFA-323, and VMF(AW)-451. *CG FMFLant 292246Z in G-3 Jnl, 4th MEB ComdD*

At 1811R, the first C-130s carrying men of the 3d Brig, 82d AbnDiv lifted from Pope AFB, while planes were airborne, the JCS directed their diversion to DomRep for air landing at San Isidro. *CinCLant Resume*

At 1858R, the JCS assigned the unclassified code name POWER PACK to U.S. operations in DomRep. *JCS 292158Z in MCCC Items*

At 1912R, CJTF 122 dissolved TG 44.9 and activated TF 124 in its stead. *CTF 124 300210Z in CJTF 122 Rpt*

At 1945R, flight operations of HMM-264 were secured after approximately 375 evacuees had been lifted from LZ 4 to ships of TF 124. *BLT 3/6 ComdD; ProvMAG-60 ComdD*

At 2007R, Commander Air Force Task Force 121 (CTF 121) notified CinCLant that his CP was in operation at Ramey AFB. *CinCAFStrike 300107Z in CJTF 122 Rpt*

At 2313R, CG FMFLant advised BuMed of the strong possibility of an augmentation request for at least six medical officers for DomRep. *CG FMFLant 300413Z in MCCC Items*

30Apr65   At 0108R, CJTF 122 informed CinCLant of his initial concept of operations, calling for the 3d Brig, 82d AbnDiv to secure San Isidro, the road to Santo Domingo, and the Duarte Bridge over the Ozama River; 6th MEU to establish an International Safety Zone (ISZ) including the AmEmb; and for DomRep Loyalist forces to patrol between the two American perimeters. American forces to use no weapons larger than small arms without permission of higher headquarters. *CJTF 122 300608Z in CJTF 122 Rpt*

At 0146R, CinCLant recommended that CJTF 122 designate CG 82d AbnDiv as commander of all American ground forces in DomRep (CTF 120) *CinCLant 300646Z in CJTF 122 Rpt*

At 0200R, the Council of the Organization of American States (OAS) passed a resolution calling on all parties in DomRep to make every effort for a cease fire and directing the setting up of an ISZ encompassing the embassy area; the JCS in transmitting this information gave CJTF 122 authority to use necessary forces to establish an ISZ including the Hotel Embajador and AmEmb. *JCS 300854Z in CJTF 122 Rpt*

At 0230R, transports carrying the 3d Brig, 82d AbnDiv began landing at San Isidro; CG 82d AhnDiv designated CTF 120 by CJTF 122 *Tompkins, Ubique*

At 0750R, CJTF 122 requested CinCLant to deploy the rest of 1/6 to DomRep and indicated a need for an additional helo squadron. *CJTF 122 301250Z in CJTF 122 Rpt*

At 0810R, the JCS directed CinCLant to move the remaining BCTs of the 82d AbnDiv to DomRep as soon as possible. *JCS 301310Z in MCCC Items*

At 0845R, two UH-34s of HMM-264 were sent to San Isidro on 48-hour loan for use of CTF 120. *ProvMAG-60 ComdD*

At 0930R, at a White House conference, the President ordered the Chairman, JCS to commit the 4th MEB and the entire 82d AbnDiv to DomRep, with the 101st AbnDiv prepared to follow. *Palmer Rpt*

At 0945R, CO 6th MEU ordered CO BLT 3/6 to advance to Phase Line CAIRO, the boundary of the ISZ and to set up defenses along Calle Navarro and Calle Sanchez which included the AmEmb within the protected zone; the advance began at 1130R and all companies were on their objective within an hour; light rebel sniper fire was received on both flanks. *BLT 3/6 ComdD*

In mid-morning, after leaving a security detachment at San Isidro, the 3d Brig, 82d AbnDiv advanced toward Duarte Bridge encountering light sniper fire on the bridge approaches and suffering four men WIA during attack to clear this opposition. *CG 82dAbnDiv 302000Z in CJTF 122 Rpt*

At 1100R, Alpha increment of 1/6 completed unloading at Jaina and moved to LZ 4-Embajador area; CO 6th MEU placed the unit under opcon of CO BLT 3/6. *CJTF 122 301640Z in CJTF 122 Rpt; BLT 3/6 ComdD*

At 1304R, the JCS directed CinCLant to activate Headquarters, XVIII ABnCorps (minus) and move it to San Isidro and to place the remaining BCTs of 82d AbnDiv on DefCon 3. *JCS 301804Z in CJTF 122 Rpt*

At 1318R, CinCLantFlt directed ComPhibLant to sail an LPH to Onslow Beach to embark a reinforced battalion and a helo squadron; CG FMFLant was directed to embark these units. *CinCLantFlt 30181SZ in CJTF 122 Rpt*

At 1452R, CinCLantFlt directed ComPhibLant to sail PhibRons 8 and 12 to Morehead City/Onslow Beach to embark sea tail of 4th MEB; message indicated that BLT 1/2 was substituted for BLT 2/2, slated for the Mediterranean in June. *CinCLantFlt 301952Z in CJTF 122 Rpt; MCCC Items*

At 1517R, CG 2d MarDiv designated BLT 1/8 for airlift alert duty in place of BLT 1/6. *CG 2d MarDiv 302017Z in G-3 Jnl, 4th MEB ComdD*

Shortly after 1500R, as I/3/6 attempted to move from Checkpoint CHARLIE, on the left flank of Phase Line CAIRO, to its next objective, DELTA, it came under heavy fire from rebel snipers with four WIA in the ensuing action; about 1530R CO I/3/6 received permission to employ 3.5-inch rocket launchers and dispersed the snipers. *BLT 3/6 ComdD*

About 1600R, continuing the advance to objective DELTA, a platoon of I/3/6 supported by a tank and two LVTs again came under heavy rebel fire; one man KIA and four WIA before company CO ordered withdrawal to Checkpoint CHARLIE; CO BLT 3/6 recommended that DELTA not be occupied at this time and CO 6th MEU concurred. *6th MEU ComdD*

About 1630R, a cease fire agreement was signed at the San Isidro headquarters of the Loyalist junta by the Papal Nuncio acting for the rebels, junta representatives, the U.S. Ambassador, and CTF 120 for CJTF 122; the agreement asked the OAS to send a commission to arbitrate the conflict. *Tompkins, Ubique*

At day's end, BLT 3/6 had consolidated its positions along Phase Line CAIRO; Marine casualties for the day's fighting were 1 KIA and 16 WIA; 40-50 rebel casualties were estimated with 3 confirmed KIA. *BLT 3/6 ComdD*

Remaining combat elements of BLT 3/6 (Ontos platoon, Reconnaissance platoon, and E/2/10) came ashore during the day and moved to the LZ 4 - Embajador perimeter; Ontos platoon moved forward to support I/3/6 prior to nightfall *BLT 3/6 ComdD*

At 1810R, CG FMFLant directed CG 2d MarDiv and CG 2d MAW to embark BLT 1/2 and HMM-263 by helo off Onslow Beach at first light on 1 May. *CG FMFLant 302310Z in CJTF 122 Rpt*

By 1900R, all loyalist forces in the Duarte Bridge area had been relieved by 82d AbnDiv elements; Army casualties of the day's fighting were 5 WIA; 8 rebel KIA and 8 WIA were estimated with 2 prisoners. *CG 82d AbnDiv 302000R in CJTF 122 Rpt*

At 1900R, airlift echelon of Headquarters, 4th MEB left Camp Lejeune, arriving at Cherry Point at 2105R, for airlift to DomRep on 1 May. *4th MEB ComdD*

At 2000R, a platoon of the 82d AbnDiv, helo lifted from San Isidro, reported to opcon of CO BLT 3/6 and was assigned part of the LZ 4 - Embajador perimeter defenses. *BLT 3/6 ComdD*

At 2345R, CG XVIII AbnCorps arrived at San Isidro with elements of his headquarters group. *ComLanForDomRep 020038Z in CJTF 122 Rpt*

1May65   At 0202R, the JCS directed the movement of additional medical units to DomRep to help cope with the civilian casualties and overtaxed military medical facilities, by day's end 5 emergency medical teams and 30,000 pounds of medical supplies were in DomRep. *JCS 010602Z in JCS 2338/13-3*

At 0430R, in a heavy exchange of fire with the rebels, I/3/6 at Checkpoint CHARLIE had 1 KIA, 1 WIA. *BLT 3/6 ComdD*

At 0612R, the JCS directed CinCLant to deploy the remainder of BLT 1/6 and two BCTs, 82d AbnDiv by air to DomRep. *JCS 011112Z in CJTF 122 Rpt*

At 0846R, VMFA-323 and VMF(AW)-451 chopped to opcon of 4th MEB from ComCaribSeaFron. *VMFA-323 ComdD; VMF(AW)-451 ComdD*

At 1054R, in accordance with a JCS directive, CinCLant ordered activation of ArLant and AFLant commands to control Army and Air Force component operations in connection with the buildup of forces in DomRep. These commands paralleled CinCLantFlt. *CinCLant 011554Z in CinCLant DomRep msg file*

At 1208, airlift of two BCTs, 82d AbnDiv began from Pope AFB. *CinCAFLant 061705Z in CJTF 122 Rpt*

At 1245R, according to plan, patrols from I/3/6 and 3d Brig, 82d AbnDiv linked up near Checkpoint CHARLIE; Army units suffered 2 KIA and 5 WIA from rebel fire during the move; about 1315R, both patrols were ordered to return to their original positions by CTF 120. *BLT 3/6 ComdD, Tompkins, Ubique*

At 1242R, the initial airlift echelon of Headquarters, 4th MEB left Cherry Point, arriving at San Isidro at 1730R; the CG's party landed at 1900R; all bivouacked at San Isidro overnight. *4th MEB ComdD*

At 1600R, CG XVIII AbnCorps assumed command of U.S. Land Forces, DomRep, relieving CG 82d AbnDiv as CTF 120. *ComLan-ForDomRep 020038Z in CJTF 122 Rpt*

At 1815R, initial elements of BLT 1/6 arrived at San Isidro; CO reported to opcon of 6th MEU at 2045R. *1/6 ComdD; 6th MEU ComdD*

In late afternoon, in the face of a rebel threat of attack on the AmEmb during the night of 1/2 May, CO, BLT 3/6 ordered organization of a provisional company to protect the area, composed a platoon from L/3/6; a platoon from K/3/6; a platoon from H&S/3/6; and a platoon B/1/505 AbnInf which moved up from the LZ 4 - Embajador perimeters. *BLT 3/6 ComdD*

By the day's end, 4,595 Army and 2,084 Marine forces had arrived in the DomRep area. *JCS 2338/13-3*

2May65   At 0605R, last airlift elements of BLT 1/6 arrived at San Isidro. *1/6 ComdD*

At 0645R, helo operations began with two UH-34s launched from the Boxer with pathfinder elements to set up an LZ at San Isidro for lift of Headquarters 4th MEB and BLT 1/6. *ProvMAG-60 ComdD*

At 1200R, after reporting to CJTF 122 on the CA Newport News and conferring with CO 6th MEU on the *Boxer*, CG 4th MEB assumed command of all Marine Forces in the DomRep area; 6th MEU redesignated RLT-6. *4th MEB ComdD; 6th MEU ComdD*

At 1108R, in response to a JCS directive, CinCLant ordered the deployment of the 5th and 6th BCTs of the 82d AbnDiv to DomRep as soon as possible; first C-130s actually lifted from Pope AFB at 0920R. *CinCLant 021608Z* and *CinCAFLant 061705Z in CJTF 122 Rpt*

During the morning, the preloaded element of the Collecting & Clearing Company, which arrived with Headquarters, 4th MEB and BLT 1/6, was moved to Sans Souci beach east of the Ozama River to move by the *Raleigh*'s LSU to Jaina; rebels fired on the convoy, returned by Army escort, with no friendly casualties. *4th MEB ComdD*

At 1227R, ProvMAG-60 chopped to control of 4th MEB; VMFA-323 and VMF(AW)-451 were put under opcon of ProvMAG-60. *ProvMAG-60 ComdD*

At 1234R, the JCS directed CinCLant to employ all available resources in DomRep to jam rebel radio broadcasts which were taking a violently anti-American cast. *JCS 021734Z in CJTF 122 Rpt*

At 1258R, the JCS directed CinCLant to deploy remaining USAF tactical air support units held in readiness for DomRep to Ramey AFB; priority of airlift to go to movement of 82d AbnDiv elements to DomRep. *JCS 021758 in CJTF 122 Rpt*

At 1303R and at 2140R, the JCS directed CinCLant to order CTF 120 to establish a Line of Communication (LOC) between Marine and Army forces in DomRep after midnight on 2 May. *JCS 021803Z and JCS 030140Z in JCS 2338/13-3*

During the afternoon, following the arrival of BLT 1/6 in LZ 4, the Bravo Command Group of BLT 3/6 moved forward to AmEmb grounds, leaving only a supply point and E/2/10 of BLT 3/6 in the LZ area. *BLT 3/6 ComdD*

At 1630R, at the request of the Ambassador, CO 6th MEU ordered the defense line manned by K/3/6 moved east two blocks to lessen the danger to the AmEmb from rebel sniper fire *BLT 3/6 ComdD*

During the day, the Secretary General of the OAS arrived at San Isidro as the forerunner of a fiveman OAS committee which would work to end hostilities *Washington Post, 2 May 65*

After darkness fell, sniper fire hitting in L/3/6 positions wounded one Marine. *BLT 3/6 ComdD*

By 2100R, all helos were back on board the *Boxer* after having transported 1,100 passengers and 60 tons of cargo from San Isidro to LZ 4 *ProvMAG-60 ComdD*

At 2003R, CNO, in response to a CinCLantFlt request, ordered the activation of nine LSTs for DomRep supply movement, first ship to be ready to load at Norfolk on 4 May. *CNO 030103Z in MCCC Items*

At 2053R, the JCS ordered CinCLant to deploy the 7th, 8th, 9th BCTs of the 82d AbnDiv and the 1st Bn, 8th Mar to DomRep. *JCS 030103Z in CJTF 122 Rpt*

By day's end, 6,218 Army and 3,029 Marine forces had arrived in the DomRep area. *JCS 2338/13-3*

3May65   At 0100R, CG 2d MarDiv requested permission from CMC to cancel recruit leaves for men completing ITR because of commitments and alert requirements, CMC approved request at 1731R. *HQMC Readiness Staff Jnl*

At 0111R, the LOC between the 82d AbnDiv and 4th MEB was established when Army units linked up with a platoon of L/3/6 near Checkpoint CHARLIE. *JCS 2338/13-3; BLT 3/6 ComdD*

At 0230R, sea tail of 4th MEB sailed from Morehead City in ships of PhibRons 8 and 12; ETA DomRep 061400R. *CTG 44 6 031249Z in MCCC Items*

At dawn, rebel sniper fire on K/3/6 positions resulted in 1 KIA; as the volume of fire increased Co K returned it with M-14s, M-60s, and M-79s and the rebels withdrew. *BLT 3/6 ComdD*

At 0555R, the first transports lifting the 7th, 8th, and 9th BCTs of the 82d AbnDiv began leaving Pope AFB for DomRep. *CinClant 031918Z in CJTF 122 Rpt*

At 0600R, reinforced Marine Detachment of the *Newport News* began debarking, it arrived by LCM at Jaina at 0745 and moved to the ISZ, where CG 4th MEB attached it to BLT 1/6; the detachment's mission, given by CJTF 122, was to patrol and search the grounds of the University of Santo Domingo for a CIA-reported rebel arms cache. *CO MD Newport News Rpt*

About 0630R, five C-130s of VMGR-352 arrived at Cherry Point from El Toro to augment VMGR-252 for the lift of BLT 1/8 to DomRep; CinClantFlt chopped four C-130s and four C-121s to CG 2d MAW to support movement; the loan, for 24 hours, of the VMGR-352 planes was authorized by the JCS with CinCPac approval. *MCCC Items; HQMC Readiness Staff Jnl*

At 0745R, airlift of 4th MEB/BLT 1/6 personnel and supplies from San Isidro to LZ 4 continued; when flight operations were secured at 1800R, 200 passengers and 100 tons of cargo had been moved. *ProvMAG-60 ComdD*

During the morning, C/1/325 AbnInf reported to opcon of BLT 3/6 to provide security for XVIII AbnCorps CP at Trujillo Palace; the Army unit also provided a reserve for defense of the AmEmb and the platoon of B/1/505 AbnInf was released to parent control; the platoon of L/3/6 on guard at the AmEmb since 28 April was also released to parent control and replaced BLT 3/6 ReconPlat. *BLT 3/6 ComdD*

At 1130R, 4th MEB CP established at Hotel Hispaniola in the ISZ; CG 4th MEB assumed opcon of Collecting & Clearing Co (C/2d MedBn) located near Hotel Embajador. *G-3 Jnl, 4th MEB ComdD*

At 1330R, C/1/6 was returned to parent control; BLT 1/6 was assigned responsibility for the western portion of the ISZ and the security of the MSR to Jaina. *1/6 ComdD*

About 1330R, the OAS Commission, whose members had arrived in DomRep on 2 May, asked the U.S. to provide protection for the

Embassies of Equador and El Salvador which were in the rebel-controlled zone. *AmEmb SD 031830Z in JCS 2338/13-3*

About 1330R, LPH *Guadalcanal* with Co A, 229th Airmobile Bn (34 UHIE) left Jacksonville, Fla., for DomRep; this unit, which gave the 82d AbnDiv its own helo capability, arrived DomRep 060600R. *CTF 124 061840Z and FoneCon AWR 040427Q in MCCC Items*

At 1538R, CJTF 122 directed CTF 121 to control and coordinate all air operations into, within, and departing the DomRep area *CJTF 122 032038Z in JCS 2338/13-3*

At 1550R, CG FMFLant advised CG 4th MEB to unload only equipment and supplies essential to his mission and to maintain ability for "ready reembarkation in combat loaded status " *CG FMFLant 032050Z in G-3 Jnl, 4th MEB ComdD*

By the day's end, 9,227 and 4,312 Marine forces had arrived in the DomRep area *JCS 2338/13-3*

4May65   At 0120R, BLT 1/8 began flying out of Cherry Point with the initial elements arriving at San Isidro at 0520R; CO reported to opcon of 4th MEB at 0800R, entire battalion had landed by 2100R. *6th MEU ComdD; BLT 1/8 ComdD*

At 0800R, HMM-264 began transporting BLT 1/8 from San Isidro to LZ 4; by the time flight operations were secured at 1930R, about 1,200 passengers and 75 tons of cargo had been transported. *ProvMAG-60 ComdD*

At 0930R, RLT-6 CP moved ashore from the *Boxer* and was established at the Hotel Hispaniola *4th MEB ComdD*

At 1100R, *Okinawa* with BLT 1/2 and HMM-263 embarked, arrived off Santo Domingo; BLT 1/2 assigned mission of the 4th MEB reserve, prepared to land on order; HMM-263 chopped to opcon of ProvMAG-60. *BLT 1/2 ComdD; ProvMAG-60 ComdD*

At 1246R, last elements of the 7th, 8th, and 9th BCTs of the 82d AbnDiv landed at San Isidro. *CJTF 122 Rpt*

At 1415R, ComPhibLant, having arrived in the DomRep area, assumed command as CTF 124 of all naval elements of JTF 122. *ComPhibLant 041915Z in CJTF 122 Rpt*

At 1545R, on order from 4th MEB, L/3/6 advanced its lines four blocks east to include the Ecudorian and San Salvadorian Embassies; move completed by 1615R; in an abortive small-scale attack on the new positions shortly after the move, three rebels were killed. *BLT 3/6 ComdD*

At 1649R, the JCS directed CinCLant to extend U.S. lines to include the Embassies of Equador and El Salvador, confirming advices received earlier in the day. *JCS 042149Z in JCS 2338/13-3*

At 1800R, the 4th MEB assigned BLT 1/6 responsibility for the central portion of the ISZ and BLT 1/8 responsibility for the western portion and the security of the MSR to Jaina. *6th MEU ComdD*

At 1814R, CTF 120 established rigid northern and eastern boundaries to the ISZ with flexible boundaries to the west that 4th MEB could exceed to support and protect LZ 4 *CG 4th MEB 042314Z in G-3 Jnl, 4th MEB ComdD*

During the day, on order of CO BLT 3/6, a modified people-to-people program was put into effect with Marines providing food to those who needed it, particularly in the I/3/6 area which included a poorer class district. *BLT 3/6 ComdD*

During the day's operations, LSU of RLT-6 was redesignated LSG of 4th MEB; LSA No. 1 was established at LZ 4 as primary issue point for Class I, II, IV, and V supplies; BSA at Jaina provided 2d echelon maintenance support; RLT-6 provided a 60-man BSA security force under opcon of LSG commander. *4th MEB ComdD*

By the day's end, 11,554 Army and 6,142 Marine forces had arrived in the DomRep area. *JCS 2338/13-3*

5May65   At 0001R, in interim command arrangements prescribed by CinCLant, CTF 120 began reporting directly to CinCLant on a command level with CJTF 122 *CTF 120 060815Z in G-3 Jnl, 4th MEB ComdD*

At dawn, HMM-263, operating from the Okinawa, began flying in support of the landing forces; HMM-264 stood down for maintenance and crew rest *ProvMAG-60 ComdD*

At 1025R, CTF 120 directed CG 4th MEB to land BLT 1/2. *G-3 Jnl, 4th MEB ComdD*

During the morning, the ship's platoon from the *Boxer* was returned to L/3/6 after seven day's absence. *BLT 3/6 ComdD*

Because of crowded conditions near the XVIII AbnCorps CP, CO BLT 3/6 moved his CP to Luis Munoz Rivera School, right on the defense line; move completed by afternoon. *BLT 3/6 ComdD*

At 1500R, CO BLT 1/2 received verbal orders at 4th MEB CP to land his unit as soon as possible, on his return to the *Okinawa*, he found ComPhibRon 12 had received orders from CTF 124 not to land the BLT. *BLT 1/2 ComdD*

At 1509R, CG 4th MEB directed CO BLT 1/2 and CO ProvMAG-60 to helo land BLT 1/2 beginning at 060630R. *CG 4th MEB 052009Z in G-3 Jnl, 4th MEB. ComdD*

At 1514R, the JCS directed CinCLant to return all forces nominated for but not required in DomRep to DefCon 5 status *JCS 052014Z in JCS 2338/13-3*

At 1545R, CG 4th MEB recommended deferring landing of BLT 1/2 until first light on 6 May; CTF 120 approved this recommendation. *G-3 Jnl, 4th MEB ComdD*

During the afternoon, an Army vehicle which strayed out of the LOC into the rebel area escaped into Marine lines with one passenger WIA. *BLT 3/6 ComdD*

During the day, in order to maximize capabilities of available artillery, CO RLT-6 formed Battery Group Echo (E/2/10 and Howtar/3/10) in position near LZ 4. *6th MEU ComdD*

During the day, a permanent exterior AmEmb guard was established by a platoon of K/3/6. *BLT 3/6 ComdD*

By day's end, 13,053 Army and 6,142 Marine forces had arrived in the DomRep area; a total of 4,317 non-combatants (2,694 U.S. Nationals) had been evacuated. *JCS 2338/13-3*

6May65   At 0600R, Marine Detachment *Newport News* was relieved in positions at University of Santo Domingo by 81mm Mortar Platoon of BLT 1/6; detachment reported back on board ship at 0940R *CO MD Newport News Rpt*

During an early morning session, the OAS, meeting in Washington, approved a proposal that would create an Inter-American Peace Force to restore order in DomRep; the proposal was passed by the required minimum of 14 votes with 5 countries voting against it and 1 abstaining . *Washington Post, 6May65*

, About 0900R, two vehicles from Howtar/3/10, en route to San Isidro for medical/motor transport supplies, strayed into the rebel area and were fired upon; in the ensuing fire fight, three Marines were KIA and two WIA, who were later recovered and evacuated; two prisoners were returned at 1725R after negotiations by the OAS Commission. *G-3 Jnl, 4th MEB ComdD*

At 1030R, a UH1E from VMO-1 attached to HMM-263 was hit by small arms fire over rebel area; the pilot, though wounded, managed to land safely; aircraft damage was minor *ProvMAG-60 ComdD*

About 1040R, two reporters from the *Miami Herald* were wounded, one seriously, at L/3/6 checkpoint, when their car, coming from the rebel area, approached the checkpoint while it was under rebel fire and then suddenly backed away, the reporters were evacuated to the *Boxer G-3 Jnl, 4th MEB ComdD*

At 1425R, CG FMFLant requested CinCLantFlt to return VMFA-323 to Cherry Point as soon as possible in order to complete personnel transfers and stabilize the unit for WesPac deployment in September. *CG FMFLant 061925Z in MCCC Items*

At 1715R, ComNavAirLant requested CG FMFLant to chop VMF(AW)-451 to CAW-8 on 15 June to permit carrier qualification and relevant training prior to deployment to the Mediterranean on 24 August. *ComNavAirLant 062215Z in MCCC Items*

During the day, the Helo Support Team of BLT 1/2 was detached and landed to support operations ashore. *BLT 1/2 ComdD*

During the day, four US Army personnel made it safely to K/3/6 lines after they had strayed from the LOC into rebel territory. Having been fired upon, they abandoned their M-37 and commandered a civilian vehicle to escape. *BLT 3/6 ComdD*

At 2250R, CTF 124 recommended to CJTF 122 that no further combat units of the 4th MEB be landed until adequate logistical support units had been landed. *CTF 124 070350Z in G-4 Jnl, 4th MEB ComdD*

7May65   At 0700R, CinCLant placed the 101st AbnDiv on DefCon5 and chopped it to CinCStrike. *CinCLant Resume*

During the morning, 4th MEB received the first formal written operation order issued by CTF 120, confirming its principal mission as security of the ISZ. *TF 120 OpO 7-65, 062400R in G-3 Jnl, 4th MEB ComdD*

At 1200R, on CinCLant order, TF 120 and JTF 122 were dissolved and CG XVIII AbnCorps became USComDomRep reporting directly to CinCLant as commander of all forces ashore; concurrent with his assumption of command, USComDomRep designated CG 4th MEB as Commander U.S. Naval Force DomRep. *CinCLant 071820Z in CTF 122 Rpt; G-3 Jnl, 4th MEB ComdD*

At 1200R, ComSecondFlt, at CinCLant direction, turned over command of all naval forces afloat in the DomRep area to CTF 124, ComSecondFlt in *Newport News* departed for Norfolk at 1436R. *ComSecondFlt 071936Z; ComPhibLant 071431Z in CJTF 122 Rpt*

At 1204R, CG FMFLant recommended to CinCLantFlt that BLT 1/2 and HMM-263 be returned to ConUS as soon as possible, BLT 1/2, just returned from the Mediterranean on 12 March, was scheduled for phased reorganization of personnel starting 1 June; HMM-263, scheduled for deployment to WesPac, was scheduled to begin preparations on 1 July. *CG FMFLant 071704Z in G-3 Jnl, 4th MEB ComdD*

During the day, a new five-man junta, with General Imbert as its head, was established by the Loyalists as the Government of National Reconstruction (GNR). *JCS 2338/13-3*

At 1700R, airlift grand total for the deployment of POWER PACK forces to DomRep was 1,857 sorties, 16,050 tons of cargo, and 19,842 passengers. *CinCLant Resume*

At 1808R, CinCLantFlt designated CG 4th MEB as CTG 124.8, Commander Landing Force in TF 124 *CTF 124 080434Z in G-3 Jnl, 4th MEB ComdD*

At 1838R, CinCLant directed CTF 124 to release VMFA-323 to normal operational control as soon as possible. *CinCLant 072338Z in MCCC Items*

At 1929R, CG 2d MarDiv recommended to CG FMFLant the following withdrawal order in any withdrawal directed prior to 1 June: (1) BLT 1/2; (2) 1/8 (Rein); (3) 1/6 (Rein); (4) 4th MEB and supporting headquarters; (5) BLT 3/6 (6th MEU) to resume as Carib Ready Force. *CG 2d MarDiv 080029Z in MCCC Items*

8May65 About 0047R, an estimated five rebels attempted to infiltrate the BSA at Jaina and were driven off after a brief fire fight; during the action one Marine was WIA, later DOW. *G-3 Jnl, 4th MEB ComdD*

At 1300R, VMFA-323 was returned to opcon of CG 2d MAW; in its 10-day participation in POWER PACK, the squadron flew 166 sorties, including 26 CAP and 140 low level reconnaissance. *VMFA-323 ComdD*

During the day, supporting units of 4th MEB, embarked in ships of PhibRons 8 and 12, began landing at Jaina and were attached to RLT-6 and LSG. *G-4 Jnl, 4th MEB ComdD*

At 1822R, CinCLant submitted his views to the JCS on force requirements in DomRep; regarding order of withdrawal, he believed it desirable to withdraw Marines as soon as it was militarily and politically feasible. *CinCLant 082322Z in MCCC Items*

9May65 At 0820R, first elements of BLT 1/8 began relieving units of BLT 3/6 in a phased exchange of positions completed at 1350R. *BLT 1/8 ComdD; BLT 3/6 ComdD*

10May65 At 1000R, two UH-34s of HMM-264 flew cross island from the *Boxer* to the north coast on a reconnaissance mission for possible arms smuggling; they remained overnight on the *Raleigh*, cruising off the north coast, returning in the early afternoon of the 11th. *ProvMAG-60 ComdD*

During the day, CO 2/10 assumed command of all artillery units ashore with his CP near the Hotel Embajador. *2/10 ComdD*

During the day, a 4th MEB Detainee Compound was established near LZ 4 in LSA No. 1; prior to this time detainees were not held by 4th MEB. *4th MEB ComdD*

11May65 During the day, ProvMAG-60 CP and Air Control Element moved from LZ 4 to San Isidro to function as a Tactical Air Direction Center. *ProvMAG-60 ComdD*

12May65	At 1430R, in accordance with RLT-6 orders, approved by USCom-DomRep, BLT 1/8 moved forward to straighten its lines facing the rebel area; move was completed by 1630R amidst quickening sniper fire. *BLT 1/8 ComdD*

At 1852R, a rebel sniper killed one Marine at BLT 1/6 checkpoint. *G-1 Jnl, 4th MEB ComdD*

13May65	At 1259R, USComDomRep advised CinCLant that time had come to seize the main rebel radio station, source of bitter anti-American propaganda; U.S. Ambassador advised approval of plan to seize station by widening western end of the LOC. *USComDomRep 131757Z in MCCC Items*

At 1420R, four F-51s of the DomRep Air Force attacked main rebel radio station, temporarily knocking it off the air; rounds from this unannounced strafing attack fell in the BLT 1/8 area. *4th MEB ComdD; CAFTF 121 132025Z in MCCC Items*

About 1500R, engineer bath unit and air delivery personnel of BLT 1/2 were landed at Jaina to reinforce LSG *CO Trps Waldo County 132055Z in BLT 1/2 ComdD*

14May65	During the morning, an RF8A of VMCJ-2, attached to VMF(AW)-451, was pursued while on a photo mission by a DomRep F-51; the Marine plane accelerated out of contact, thereafter, all photo missions had an armed F8D escort. *VMF(AW)-451 ComdD*

At 1400R, with the arrival of a Honduran rifle company at San Isidro, Operation PRESS AHEAD, the deployment of Latin American contingents to the Inter-American Peace Force began. *G-3 Jnl, 4th MEB ComdD*

During the day, a 4th MEB Engineer Group was formed to assure accomplishment of construction tasks incident to a prolonged stay in DomRep. *4th MEB ComdD*

During the day, 4th MEB unit galleys began feeding B rations to all personnel except those in small units in isolated locations. *4th MEB ComdD*

At 1952R, CTF 124, in response to an oral request from USCom-DomRep, directed ComPhibRon 12 (CTG 124.7) to provide one platoon of BLT 1/2 for security of the dock area adjacent to the SS

Mallory Lykes during unloading from 151200R to 182400R. *CTF 124 150052Z in BLT 1/2 ComdD*

15May65   About 0549R, a Marine in the BLT 1/8 area was slightly wounded by rebel sniper fire, treated, and returned to duty. *S-1 Jnl, BLT 1/B ComdD*

During the morning, CTG 124.7 landed one platoon of BLT 1/2 to provide dock security for the SS *Mallory Lykes*. *4th MEB ComdD*

With the start of the day's helo operations, HMM-264 began taking duty in LZ 4 every day and every other night in order that HMM-263 could conduct training flights. *HMM-264 ComdD*

At 1012R, CG 4th MEB, in regard to the landing of the BLT 1/2 platoon, informed CTF 124 that no air or ground element of 4th MEB should be committed to any task without prior approval of CG 4th MEB; CG FMFLant confirmed this interpretation to CinCLantFlt and other addressees on 17 May. *CG 4th MEB 151512Z and CG FMFLant 172345Z in BLT 1/2 ComdD*

During the day, a detachment from 2d Radio Battalion reported to 4th MEB with equipment to set up a CritiCom Terminal; circuit established with Director Naval Security Group, Atlantic by 161700R. *4th MEB ComdD*

16May65   During the day, CinCLant chopped all except six C-130s back to CinCStrike; the six were retained for support of POWER PACK and PRESS AHEAD operations. *CinCLant Resume*

During the day, USComDomRep, in order to demonstrate U.S. forces adherence to neutrality, ordered all units to cease use of loyalist soldiers at checkpoints and roadblocks, but allowed use of DomRep police if they were wearing distinctive grey uniforms *4th MEB ComdD*

During the day, USComDomRep published emergency medical evacuation procedures designed to provide a quick response anywhere in the area of operations; procedures were recorded on 3X5" cards and distributed to all 4th MEB units. *4th MEB ComdD*

During the day, 4th MEB began to reconstitute operational reserve material on board the *Boxer* from supplies ashore. *G-4 Jnl, 4th MEB ComdD*

17May65   On RLT-6 order, the ship's platoon from L/3/6 returned to the *Boxer BLT 3/6 ComdD*

As a result of GNR forces operations against rebel forces north of the ISZ, a threat of stray rounds falling into Marine positions occurred; to rectify this situation, BLT 1/8 was directed to provide a liaison officer to USComDomRep for attachment to GNR forces to insure no conflict between GNR forces and Marines by coordinating GNR activities with Marine front lines to the north. *4th MEB ComdD*

During the day, the peak strength of U.S. Forces in DomRep was reached: 14,889 Army, 7,958 Marine; and 1,000 Air Force. *JCS 2338/13-3*

18May65   About 1700R, two Marines of the 4th MEB Engineer Group inadvertently drove a civilian water truck into the rebel area, where they were fired on with 1 KIA and 1 WIA; the wounded man was recovered by a Peace Corps representative on 19 May; the body was returned by the rebels at 191810R. *G-1 Jnl, 4th MEB ComdD*

19May65   At 1315R, the SS *Mallory Lykes* was underway from Jaina; the security platoon from BLT 1/2 was withdrawn. *4th MEB ComdD*

During the day, the 4th MEB staff effected liaison with 82d AbnDiv staff to work out fire support coordination procedures in the event that use of air, artillery, or naval gunfire was authorized to support U.S. forces. *4th MEB ComdD*

20May65   During the morning, HMM-263 provided all support and standby aircraft, while HMM-264 had all its 24 helicopters in a morning flyby that logged the 50,000th accident-free flight hour over a period of 4 1/2 years. *HMM-264 ComdD, ProvMAG-60 ComdD*

Following directions issued by USComDomRep on 19 May, the Honduran and Nicaraguan detachments destined for the Inter-American Force (IAF) were quartered in the 4th MEB area, with 4th MEB acting as host unit and providing logistic support, but not exercising tactical control *4th MEB ComdD*

21May65   At 1030R, 200 women marched through the ISZ to the Embajador Hotel in an orderly protest of foreign intervention in DomRep; the group dispersed about 1140R without incident *4th MEB ComdD*

21May65 At 1200R, a 24-hour cease fire agreement, signed by both the rebels and the GNR, took effect; its purpose was to evacuate casualties and care for the dead after five days of heavy fighting in the area north of the ISZ-LOC. *4th MEB ComdD*

22May65 At 2040R, the U.S. Ambassador advised the Secretary of State that the Marine BLT already afloat could be withdrawn immediately for employment elsewhere; he also advised that a second BLT could be withdrawn, at least to ships offshore, on the arrival of the Brazilian contingent to the IAF, CinCLant concurred at 2250. *AmEmb SD 230140Z in MCCC Items*

23May65 At 0645R, the Act establishing the IAF was signed in Washington by representatives of Brazil, Costa Rica, Honduras, Nicaragua, and the United States and the Secretary General of the OAS; Brazil named General Hugo Panasco Alvim as Commander, IAF. *Cin-CLant 242028Z in MCCC Items*

During the day, a 22-man Brazilian advance party arrived in the ISZ and was quartered near other IAF units hosted by the 4th MEB. *4th MEB ComdD*

24May65 At 1540R, USComDomRep recommended to the Secretary of Defense a troop list for withdrawal from DomRep, which included two BLTs and HMM-263 (5,110 troops in all, including 3,500 Marines). *USComDomRep 242040Z in MCCC Items*

25May65 During the day, a peaceful demonstration by approximately 200 women was conducted in ISZ, ending at the Embajador Hotel; its apparent cause was OAS inaction. *4th MEB ComdD*

At 1726R, CTF 124 directed CTG 124.7 to begin transfer of necessary operational reserve material to ComPhibRon 10 shipping, preparatory to the reconstitution of Carib 2-65. *CTF 124 252226Z in G-4 Jnl, 4th MEB ComdD*

At 1810R, CTF 124 directed CTF 124.7 to reembark 700 personnel of BLT 3/6 on the *Boxer*, beginning at 260800R. *CTF 124 252310Z in G-4 Jnl, 4th MEB ComdD*

26May65 At 0015R, CG 4th MEB requested CTF 124 land service support elements to replace those loading out with reconstituted 6th MEU. *CG 4th MEB 260551Z in G-4 Jnl, 4th MEB ComdD*

At 0400R, BLT 1/6 began evacuating the grounds of Santo Domingo University and relieving units of BLT 3/6; relief completed by 0900R; evacuation completed by 1730R. *BLT 3/6 ComdD; 4th MEB ComdD*

At 0800R, elements of BLT 3/6 began helo reembarkation on the *Boxer;* BLT CP opened on board at 1000R. *4th MEB ComdD*

At 1230R, USComDomRep advised CinCLant that he was carrying out SecDef instructions to outload and withdraw the entire complement of BLT 3/6 from DomRep. *USComDomRep 261730Z in MCCC Items*

At 1610R, the JCS authorized CinCLant to return BLT 1/2 and HMM-263 and related amphibious shipping in which they were embarked to ConUS. *JCS 262110Z in MCCC Items*

At 1800R, BLT 1/2 and HMM-263, embarked in *Okinawa*, departed for ConUS; remainder of BLT elements remained on board ship in DomRep area under 4th MEB control. *BLT 1/2 ComdD*

27May65 At 1200R, CG 4th MEB assumed control of all RLT-6 forces not a part of the original 6th MEU. *4th MEB ComdD*

About 1430R, RLT-6 Co opened on board the *Boxer* after displacing from the Hotel Hispaniola. *6th MEU ComdD*

During the day, elements of BLT 1/2, including detachments of 2d FSR, 2d ServBn, 2d SP Bn, and NBG-2, were landed to replace like elements lost through the reembarkation of BLT 3/6. *BLT 1/2 ComdD; 4th MEB ComdD*

28May65 During the day, the USS *La Salle* departed DomRep for ConUS with the following Marine units: Det, HqCo, 6th Mar; HqBtry(-), 2/10; Det, MAS 1; Det, C/2d MedBn, Hq, B/2d TkBn; Hq, B/2d AT Bn; and A/2d MedBn; these units arrived and debarked at Morehead City 31 May. *2/10 ComdD, 4th MEB ComdD*

At 1905R, CG 4th MEB directed that all road barriers, check point frames, and wood frame structures for galleys and heads in the 4th MEB area be left in place for relieving 82d AbnDiv troops; all foxholes and emplacements were to be filled prior to relief. *CG 4th MEB 290005Z in G-4 Jnl, 4th MEB ComdD*

29May65 At 0600R, *Okinawa* arrived off Onslow Beach and the helo lift of BLT 1/2 ashore began; by 1230R, all battalion personnel, supplies, and equipment had been landed; by 1330R, all HMM-263 men and equipment had been landed. *BLT 1/2 ComdD, ComPhibRon 12 291834Z in G-4 Jnl, 4th MEB ComdD*

At 1410R, General Alvim assumed command of the IAF, receiving the OAS colors from USComDomRep, his deputy commander *AmEmb SD 300230 in MCCC Items*

During the day, 1,552 Army troops begin redeployment to ConUS by air; Latin American Brigade (LAB) of the IAF increased to 1,345 with the arrival of 299 more Brazilian troops. *CinCLant Resume*

Adverse weather during the day prohibited reembarkation of additional Marine units; total Carib 2-65 forces embarked in PhibRon 10 shipping was 1,046. *4th MEB ComdD*

30May65 At 1215R, RLT-6 was redesignated 6th MEU and ProvMAG-60 reverted to 6th MEU control *6th MEU ComdD*

By 1300R, ProvMAG-60 had reembarked all personnel and equipment on *Boxer*. Detachment, Air Delivery Platoon and Detachment, MABS-27 to opcon of 4th MEB *ProvMAG-60 ComdD*

At 1843R, the JCS issued a warning order to CinCLant to return all remaining POWER PACK Marine units and associated shipping to normal operations within 24 to 48 hours; assigned organic Navy and Marine and opportune Air Force airlift was to be used for the withdrawal *JCS 302343Z in MCCC Items*

During the day, reembarkation of 6th MEU completed except for troops and equipment assigned to USS *Rankin 4th MEB ComdD*

At 2256R, ComPhibLant, in response to a requirement for additional lift from CG 4th MEB, ordered one large LST sailed from Norfolk by 010800R to backload equipment and personnel. *ComPhibLant 310356Z in G-4 Jnl, 4th MEB ComdD*

31May65 At 0236R, USComDomRep advised CinCLant that he had met with General Alvim to discuss withdrawal of Marine units; General Alvim was reluctant to lose Marine combat vehicles but agreed to the withdrawal when it was explained that a BLT and a helo squadron would remain afloat under CTF 124 for emergency recall *USComDomRep 310636Z in MCCC Items*

At 1242R, CG 4th MEB notified USComDomRep that the Marine bulk fuel detachment and equipment at Jaina which was pumping fuel to commercial storage facilities from ships would be withdrawn about 3 June unless otherwise directed. *CG 4th MEB 311742Z in G-4 Jnl, 4th MEB ComdD*

At 2029R, USComDomRep requested CTF 124 to transfer accountability of Marine bulk fuel equipment to an appropriate agency as it was "vital to the needs of this command." *USComDomRep 010129Z in G-4 Jnl, 4th MEB ComdD*

At 1956R, CTF 124 directed CG 4th MEB to leave bulk fuel men and equipment in place until no longer needed *CTF 124 010056Z in G-4 Jnl, 4th MEB ComdD*

At 2400R, VMF(AW)-451 was returned to opcon of ComCarib-SeaFron; during DomRep operations it had flown 726.7 hours, including 232 CAP missions, 34 photo escort missions, 115 road reconnaissance missions, 6 beach reconnaissance missions. *VMF-(AW)-451 ComdD*

1Jun65   Beginning at 0800R, 4th MEB relieved of responsibility for that portion of the ISZ held by BLT 1/8; BLT 1/8 relieved in place by elements of the 82d AbnDiv and moved to Jaina to begin embarking. *BLT 1/8 ComdD; 4th MEB ComdD*

2Jun65   At 0955R, CG 4th MEB submitted airlift requirements to CG 2d MAW for three C-130s, one each on 3, 5, and 6 June, to transport advance echelons of units returning to ConUS. *CG 4th MEB 021455Z in G-4 Jnl, 4th MEB ComdD*

At 1100R, 6th MEU was chopped to control of ComPhiRon 10 as TU 45 9 of the reconstituted Carib 2-65. *4th MEB ComdD*

During the day, two companies of Brazilian troops passed through U.S. lines to secure a demilitarized zone around the GNR-held National Palace in the rebel area. *CinCLant Resume*

At 2000R, CG 4th MEB reported to CG FMFLant that final arrangements for bulk fuel pumping support had been made with the equipment to remain under Navy control until no longer needed; all 2d FSR personnel were to return to ConUS. *CG 4th MEB 030100Z in G-4 Jnl, 4th MEB ComdD*

3Jun65	During the day, BLT 1/8 completed embarkation and sailed for ConUS. *BLT 1/8 ComdD*

At 1955R, USComDomRep informed CG 4th MEB that President Johnson had announced that all Marines would be withdrawn from DomRep in accordance with General Alvim's statement that conditions permitted such withdrawal. *G-3 Jnl, 4th MEB ComdD*

At 2335R, CinCLant directed the 82d AbnDiv to relieve 4th MEB by 041600R and the 4th MEB to prepare for reembarkation of Hq, 4th MEB, BLT 1/6, and supporting elements. *CinCLant 040435Z in MCCC Items*

4Jun65	At 0747R, the JCS directed CinCLant to return to normal operations all remaining Marine units and associated shipping deployed for DomRep operations. *JCS 041247Z in MCCC Items*

At 1200R, the 82d AbnDiv relieved 4th MEB of responsibility for security of the ISZ; at 1300R, the 82d AbnDiv relieved 4th MEB of all other specific security missions. *4th MEB ComdD*

By 1345R, BLT 1/6 had been relieved in place by 82d AbnDiv units; BLT received orders to begin embarkation at 1800R and by 2340R all troops were on board except B/1/6, which was policing the BLT assembly area, and the BSA security platoon from C/1/6. *BLT 1/6 ComdD*

At 2158, USComDomRep directed CG 4th MEB to complete reembarkation of all units from DomRep and relieved 4th MEB of its last major tactical responsibility as USComDomRep reserve; local security responsibility for the BSA would continue until reembarkation was completed. *USComDomRep 050258Z in G-3 Jnl, 4th MEB ComdD*

5Jun65	By 0500R, all vehicles and supplies of BLT 1/6 were loaded, all personnel were on board by 1145R; BLT 1/6 sailed from DomRep at 1330R. *BLT 1/6 ComdD*

6Jun65	During the day, ComPhibGru 4 relieved ComPhibLant as CTF 124. *CinCLant Resume*

During the day, BLT 1/8 disembarked at Morehead City and moved to Camp Lejeune. *BLT 1/8 ComdD*

At 1500R, reembarkation of 4th MEB surface lift completed. *G-4 Jnl, 4th MEB ComdD*

At 1545R, final airlift of 4th MEB headquarters elements, CG and remaining staff, departed San Isidro; Marine personnel remaining in DomRep consisted of two officers and two enlisted men of 6th MEU claims investigating team and seven enlisted men of an air freight detachment. *4th MEB ComdD*

At 2030R, CG 4th MEB arrived at Camp Lejeune; 4th MEB CP opened at 2200R. *FoneCon FMFLant 062200R in MCCC Items; 4th MEB ComdD*

At the end of Marine participation in DomRep operations, total cumulative casualty totals of 6th MEU and 4th MEB were: KIA-1 officer, 7 enlisted (USMC), 1 enlisted (USN); WI_3 officers, 26 enlisted (USMC), 1 enlisted (USN); NBC_3 officers, 57 enlisted (USMC), 3 enlisted (USN). *G-1 Jnl, 4th MEB ComdD*

8Jun65 During the day, TG 44 9, with 6th MEU embarked, got underway for San Juan and St Thomas. *6th MEU ComdD*

9Jun65 At 0630R, BLT 1/6 arrived at Morehead City and offloaded for Camp Lejeune. *BLT 1/6 ComdD*

9-16Jun65 During this period, 6th MEU conducted extensive equipment and vehicle maintenance during liberty visits to San Juan and St. Thomas. *6th MEU ComdD*

14Jun65 At 2100R, CinCLant DomRep War Room was deactivated; its activities were assumed by CinCLant. *NMCC 142225Q in MCCC Items*

17-21
Jun65 During this period, an aggressor group and three rifle companies of BLT 3/6 conducted company training ashore on Vieques. *BLT 3/6 ComdD*

20-22
Jun65 During this period, ships and men of Carib 2-65 made liberty calls at San Juan and St. Thomas. *BLT 3/6 ComdD*

23Jun65 At 0800R, TG 44.9 sailed from Puerto Rico for ConUS. *Prov-MAG-60 ComdD; 6th MEU ComdD*

26Jun65   At 1500R, Carib 2-65 was relieved at sea by Carib 3-65. *6th MEU ComdD*

28Jun65   At 0600R, 6th MEU began landing over Onslow Beach, at Morehead City, and by helo to LZ at Camp Lejeune. *BLT 3/6 ComdD; 6th MEU ComdD*

30Jun65   During the day, BLT 3/6 was disbanded at Camp Lejeune and detachments returned to parent control. *BLT 3/6 ComdD*

9Jul65   According to instructions from CG 2d MarDiv, 6th MEU was deactivated. *CG 2d MarDiv 221638Z in 6th MEU ComdD*

Appendix E

NAVY UNIT COMMENDATION

THE SECRETARY OF THE NAVY
Washington

The Secretary of the Navy takes pleasure in commending the following commands and units:

Commander and Staff Amphibious Squadron TEN
Tactical Air Control Squadron TWENTY-TWO, Detachment INDIA
USS BOXER (LPH-4) with nucleus JT-122 Staff embarked
USS FORT SNELLING (LSD-30)
USS RALEIGH (LPD-1)
USS WOOD COUNTY (LST-1178)
USS RUCHAMKIN (APD-89)
USS YANCY (AKA-93)
USS RANKIN (AKA-103)
6th Marine Expeditionary Unit
Marine Corps Security Guard, American Embassy, Santo Domingo

for service as set forth in the following

CITATION.

For exceptionally meritorious service from 26 through 30 April 1965 in connection with the Dominican Republic crisis. Arriving off the coast of Santo Domingo on 26 April 1965, ships and Marines of Amphibious Squadron TEN commenced the mass embarkation and evacuation of over 1,000 United States civilian nationals and other refugees, among whom were large numbers of women and children from the Dominican Republic. As the situation on shore worsened, Commander Joint Task Force-122 landed combat Marines of the 6th Marine Expeditionary Unit to guarantee the safety of evacuees and for the protection of U.S. and foreign property. This major amphibious operation, introducing the first combat troops into the Dominican Republic, was smoothly conducted and all objectives achieved with minimal loss of life. The fact that the entire evacuation and troop landing operations were successfully conducted in the face of unusual conditions and obstacles, is a tribute to the dedication of all personnel involved and was in keeping with the highest traditions of the United States Naval Service.

All personnel attached to and serving on board any of the above designated units during the period 26 through 30 April 1965 are here by authorized to wear the Navy Unit Commendation Ribbon.

Secretary of the Navy

CARIBBEAN AREA

MILES

ATLANTIC OCEAN

BAHAMA ISLANDS

Grand Abaco
Great Abaco
Eleuthera Island
Cat Island
D'San Salvador
Rum Cay
Long Island
Acklins Island
Little Inagua Island
Mayaguana Island
Caicos Islands
Great Inagua Island

PUERTO RICO
San Juan
Isla de Vieques

DOMINICAN REPUBLIC
Santo Domingo
HAITI
Port-au-Prince

CARIBBEAN SEA

VENEZUELA
Caracas

COLUMBIA

GULF OF MEXICO

FLORIDA
Cape Kennedy
Miami
Tampa

CUBA
Havana
Isla de Pinos
Cayman Islands
Santiago de Cuba
Guantanamo

JAMAICA
Kingston

PANAMA
Canal Zone
Panama

COSTA RICA
San Jose

MEXICO
Isla de Cozumel

BRITISH HONDURAS
Belize

HONDURAS
Tegucigalpa

NICARAGUA
Managua

EL SALVADOR
San Salvador

Guatemala

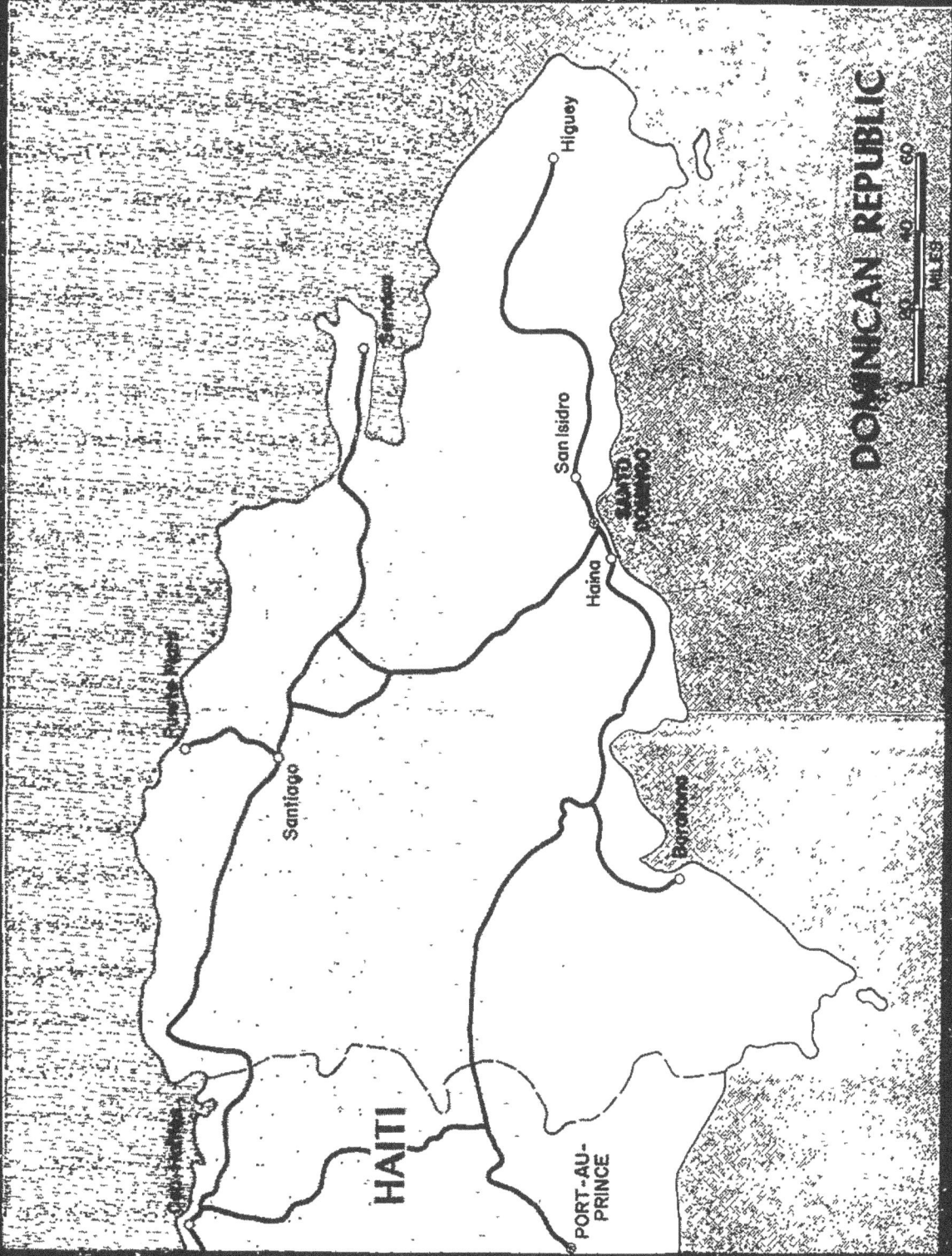

SANTO DOMINGO

––––––	Phase Line Cairo As Established By BLT 3/6 On 30 April 1965
––––––	Extension Of Phase Line Cairo By BLT 3/6 On 2 May 1965
––––––	International Safety Zone As Negotiated By Ambassador Martin On 1 May 1965
– – – –	International Safety Zone As Planned By CJTF 122
– · – · –	BLT 1/6's Position On Phase Line Cairo As Of 12 May 1965
══════	LOC As Of Night Of 2/3 May 1965.

113